India
Business

OTHER MARKETING BOOKS FROM PMP

The Kids Market: Myths & Realities

Marketing to American Latinos, Part I

Marketing to American Latinos, Part II

The Mirrored Window: Focus Groups
from a Moderator's Point of View

The Great Tween Buying Machine

Marketing Insights to Help Your Business Grow

Why People Buy Things They Don't Need

India Business

Finding Opportunities in this Big Emerging Market

Aruna Chandra,

Pradeep Rau, and

John K. Ryans, Jr.

PARAMOUNT MARKET PUBLISHING, INC.

Paramount Market Publishing, Inc.
301 S. Geneva Street, Suite 109
Ithaca, NY 14850
www.paramountbooks.com
Telephone: 607-275-8100; 888-787-8100
Facsimile: 607-275-8101

Publisher: James Madden
Editorial Director: Doris Walsh

This publication is designed to provide accurate and authoritative
information in regard to the subject matter covered. It is sold with the
understanding that the publisher is not engaged in rendering legal,
accounting, or other professional services. If legal advice or other expert
assistance is required, the services of a competent professional should
be sought.

Library of Congress Catalog Number:
Cataloging in Publication Data available
ISBN 0-9671439-0-X

Book design and composition: Paperwork

YBP2003 9/20/02
RefSr FTRE HF 1590 .15 .U5 C43 2002

Contents

Acknowledgments

THE FOLLOWING executives were most generous in sharing their time and their knowledge of India in personal interviews for this book. Their insights are quoted throughout the book, but no further notes for the interviews will appear. The companies are listed alphabetically and the dates of the interviews are given to allow the reader to understand the timeframe in which the comments were made.

3M, Mr. Walt Sheela, Managing Director, 3M India, March 15, 2001.

American Greetings, Mr. Peter Pizarro, V.P., International Business Development, August 27, 1999.

Caterpillar, Mr. Dan Dasaro, Commercial Director, Caterpillar India, April 10, 2001.

Con-Agra, Mr. Asis Sengupta. V. P. Logistics, Con-Agra India, June 6, 2001

Dana Corporation, Mr. John Shaner, V.P. Corporate Relations, August 23, 1999.

Diebold, Mr. Ken Justice, Director, Market Intelligence and Worldwide Marketing, August 31, 1999.

Ford Motor Company, Mr. John Fink, V.P. Marketing and Sales, Ford India (March 1999 to February 2001), Commercial Truck Sales and Marketing Director, (February 2001 to present), Ford Division, Ford USA, March 9, 2001.

Ford Motor Company, Mr. V. Sivaramakrishnan, General Manager, Marketing and Planning, Ford India, March 9, 2001.

Gillette Corporation, Mr. John Denham, Group Business Director, AMIE (Africa, Middle East, former Soviet Union, and the Indian sub-continent), April 5, 2001.

Goodyear, Mr. Roger Hagstrom, Director of Marketing Asia, March 2, 2001.

Hewlett-Packard, Mr. Mohan Garde, V.P. Business Development, March 6, 2001.

IBM, Mr. Murali Raman, Country Manager, IBM India, May 3, 2001.

Kellogg's, Mr. Greg Peterson, Managing Director, Asia-Pacific, April 2, 2001.

Leo Burnett, Mr. Allen Chichester, Executive Vice President, Chief Administrative Officer, Leo Burnett USA, August 11, 1999.

McDonald's Corporation, Mr. Fredrik Laurell, Director of Strategic Planning and Business Research, Asia Pacific, Middle East, and Africa Division, April 2, 2001.

Morton International, Ms. Saretta Joiner, Advertising and Sales Promotion Manager, August 12, 1999.

Owens Illinois, Mr. Ricardo Yunis, V. P. Director of Sales and Marketing International, August 23, 1999.

Pillsbury, Mr. Samir Behl, V. P. Marketing, March 28, 2001.

Procter & Gamble, Mr. Helmut Meixner, former Vice President and General Manager, Procter & Gamble Asia, February 2, 2001.

Sara Lee Corporation, Mr. Miles Greer, Executive Director, Corporate Development, August 12, 1999.

TRW Corporation, Mr. Mike Schilling, Director, Corporate Development, August 27, 1999.

Wendy's Corporation, Mr. Emil Brolich, Senior Vice President, Strategic Planning, Research, and New Product Marketing, August 20. 1999.

Whirlpool, Mr. Paul Dittmann, V.P. Global Logistics, March 2, 2001.

Wrigley's International Inc., Mr. Doug Barrier, President, International, August 11, 1999.

Xerox Corporation, Mr. Carlos Pascula, V.P. Developing Markets, March 8, 2001.

The following individuals were also most helpful in producing this book:

—Sandeep Maini, Commercial Specialist, U.S. Commercial Service, U. S. Embassy, New Delhi.

—Michael Miller, Director; Ricardo Pelaez, Senior International Trade Specialist; and Marchia Brandstadt and Sasha Petrov, International Trade Specialists, Cleveland U.S. Export Assistance Center, U. S. Department of Commerce.

—Cynthia Ryans, Professor Emeritus, Libraries and Media Services, Kent State University.

—Carolina Rubiano, Graduate Research Assistant, Kent State University.

Introduction

INDIA is in the spotlight today. It is truly one of the world's hottest markets in a positive sense.

If the 1990s marked China's highly-publicized entry into the global marketplace, it appears the first decade of the 21st century will belong to India. Not only is India the world's largest democracy with a population of one billion people, it offers a consumer middle class of somewhere between 150 and 300 million.

Further, these statistics can be coupled with the country's large English speaking population, low inflation rate, a long-standing positive growth rate and an outstanding technical higher education program. It is small wonder, therefore, that India is now attracting attention from businesses in the U.S., Canada, Europe, and Asia. Clearly, it is on the radar screen of the major multi-national corporations and internationally oriented, medium-to-small companies worldwide.

India doomsayers are prepared to cite the many historic reasons why they feel the country is unlikely to achieve its potential. To illustrate, *The Economist's* annual economic forecast publication, *The World in 2001*, uses the headline "Impossible India's Improbable Chance" to describe its potential for achieving its foreign direct investment goals. Hardly a ringing endorsement for the direction the country hopes to take.

What is interesting is that both the supporters and critics of India could be correct. The country has not been an easy market to penetrate, as Lever, IBM and Coca-Cola would attest. And, as *The Economist* headline suggests, India's weak central government has led to more decentralization to the state level. On the positive side, since few global marketers would want India-wide coverage, the shift of power to key states provides greater opportunities for U.S. firms.

India: Why and Why Not?

The list of Indian emigrants to the U.S. and Europe reads like a who's who of the leading professionals. However, not all of India's brightest have left the country and many engineers and scientists are being trained there today. In fact, India's "Silicon Triangle," which includes Bangalore, Hyderabad, and Chennai (Madras), has become home to a highly skilled workforce, and that has helped spawn many indigenous software firms.

While some see India as a market of a billion-plus people, a more realistic view reveals only a handful of major city centers where the bulk of the middle-income consumers can be found. Besides the "Silicon Triangle," these city clusters include Mumbai (Bombay), New Delhi, and Kolkata (Calcutta).

Other positives include excellent local engineering and science universities, a large English-speaking population and a high level of U.S. brand recognition, as a result of the population's close contact with family members in the U.S. While the country's per capita GNP of $488 is a little over half that of China's $909, it includes the 400 million (mainly rural) with purchasing power of less than $1 per day.

U.S. Government Attention

In 1992, the U.S. Department of Commerce (DOC) announced it would be focusing its export promotion efforts on ten developing markets that were predicted to account for 27 percent of global business by the year 2010.[1] This group included India and China, as well as South Africa, Poland, Turkey, Brazil, Argentina, Mexico, Indonesia, and South Korea and it was termed the Big Emerging Markets (BEMs). The DOC subsequently moved further in the following years to implement this BEM strategy by establishing U.S. Commercial Centers in the countries. And, it also placed high priority on building relationships between businesses in the U.S. and those in the BEMs. Such advocacy efforts by the DOC marked a significant change in the U.S. role in assisting American business.[1]

More Recent Attention

India's large population, of course, is not news. However, for many years, India was perceived by the average person as little more than a land of monsoons, poverty, and exotic temples. During this period, the country itself was so caught-up in internal political issues and bureaucracy—the legacy of British rule—that it remained relatively isolated. In fact, if India, China, and Pakistan had not been involved in a game of nuclear one upmanship, they might have received little attention at all from the world press. Of course, after September 11, 2001, the war against terrorism in Afghanistan and the increased coverage of Central and South Asia in general, focused more attention on India.

Historically, India's rules for doing business were out-of-step with those normally faced by the world business community. IBM and Coca-Cola were just two of the major multinational corporations (MNCs) that tested the waters in India, but subsequently left in the 1970s because of Indian rules regarding the control of the technology and intellectual property that drive their businesses.

Interestingly, it seems to have taken China's successful emergence in the world's marketplace to cause India to make its move. The country simply could not afford to let its neighbor—a sometimes enemy and sometimes friend—grow too powerful and create a substantial development gap. Over the years, Indian business had been protected by tariff and import regulations and some very large family firms and government-owned enterprises had developed. But these industries were not then globally competitive and could certainly not compete as India began to meet World Trade Organization (WTO) requirements to lower trade barriers. Therefore, the Indian government initiated privatization plans for a number of government-owned industries and has begun to more actively seek foreign investment. These measures coupled with the enormous successes achieved by India's information technology industries and the modernization of some family firms and professionally managed groups such as Tata, are rapidly moving Indian businesses into the world market.[2]

Beginning in the latter stages of the Clinton Administration and continuing into the Bush Administration, India has taken a more prominent place in U.S. foreign policy. This attention may result from a desire to counter China's new industrial might or it may reflect the recognition of the new opportunities in India. Either way, the stage has been set for new trade and investment opportunities for the U.S. business community. Certainly, this attention has been long deserved for a country that has provided some of the brightest U.S. business people and academic scholars.

For the U.S. business community, increased policy interests in India by the U.S. government simply highlight a growing recognition that despite India's infrastructure problems and nagging political uncertainties, a middle class that is larger than the total U.S. population has enormous potential. Clearly, the time is now for firms to strongly consider India in their future plans.

This Book

Unlike the typical guide to doing business in a foreign country, this book goes well beyond simply presenting an economic, political and cultural overview of the Indian market. In addition to our assessments of the current Indian situation and its opportunities, the book takes a strategic orientation and presents the experiences of dozens of U.S. firms in the Indian market. During 1999 and 2001, we surveyed or conducted in-depth interviews with executives from more than 50 leading U.S. firms, whose responsibilities include the Indian market.

Our primary goal was to identify winning strategies for India. We also wanted to learn how these executives viewed the Indian middle class, and we wanted to find out what day-to-day problems they encountered in the country's business environment. In addition, we wanted to find out when it is possible to employ global products and promotions in the country and which companies needed to localize their marketing effort.

Of course, we did not ignore traditional topics, such as the Indian political system, its current economic situation, or its culture. These and other issues important to those considering investing or marketing in the country, such as its infrastructure concerns and its highly publicized information technology industry, are included. Further, we have provided an Indian Overview at the end of Chapter 15 that suggests signals for U.S., Canadian, and European firms to watch in order to monitor whether India is continuing on a path that is positive for potential investors or for trading.

This book is written for decision-makers in companies interested in entering India via exporting or direct investment.

Target Readers

This book is written for decision-makers in companies interested in entering India via exporting or direct investment. It is also valuable to managers of firms already operating there who are considering expansion. Our goal is to provide an impartial overview and to include the negatives, as well as the positives, about the market.

A secondary audience for the book are those M.B.A., Executive M.B.A. and corporate training programs that have specialized courses on individual country markets. Additionally, the book could serve as a text for graduate programs that feature an "overseas experience" in India. However, we wish to emphasize that our primary target market is the global business reader. Our essential questions to those firms we interviewed or surveyed dealt with how to do business or how to market your product in India.

Resources

India is a work in progress. The country has changed dramatically in the two years it took to complete the book. Besides our interviews and survey information, we found a number of publications and periodicals to be extremely valuable in keeping current on the Indian market. These include: *Financial Times, India Today, The New York Times, The Wall Street Journal, The Washington Post, The McKinsey Quarterly, The Economist, adageglobal,* and *Marketing News.* The first three were especially valuable, as were various regional publications including the *Cleveland Plain Dealer, Akron Beacon Journal,* and *Crain's Cleveland Business.*

Certainly, India is an economy in transition and new happenings relevant to firms occur daily. Thus, we recommend supplementing this book with current news items from the above publications and information from the U.S. DOC's Commercial Service in New Delhi. The latter is a "gem" and its address and e-mail/website/telephone contact information are provided in the Appendix. It is important to remember that the U.S. Department of Commerce and your nearest U.S. DOC Export Trade Assistance Center are important sources for information and local contacts in India.

The Authors

Highly experienced in international business, Drs. Rau and Chandra were born in India and have extensive experience working there. Drs. Ryans and Rau are co-authors of the widely read book, *Marketing Strategies for the New Europe,* which was published just prior to the 1992 opening of the now European Union. Collectively, these authors have served as an international business or marketing consultant for scores of companies (large and small) in the U.S. and overseas and has published widely in the field. Articles by one or more of them have appeared in the *Harvard Business Review, Business Horizons,* the *Journal of World Business,* and many others.

Lastly, this book is designed to answer the primary questions that any firm must address when considering a market. It is suggested that you read the book in the chapter order that it is presented to get the maximum benefit from it. Several chapters build on the preceding ones and the final chapter raises (and answers) the final questions we predict the reader will have after reading the entire book. We wish you, the reader "good luck" as you explore one of the world's most frustrating, intriguing, and high-potential markets remaining today.

NOTES

1. "The National Export Strategy: Annual Report to the U.S. Congress," *Business America,* Vol. 115, No. 9, p. 60.

2. "The National Export Strategy," *The Magazine of International Trade,* Vol. 117, No. 9, September 1996, p. 17.

CHAPTER 1

Speaking from Experience: 3M India

This case study is based on an interview with Mr. Walt Scheela, Managing Director (1995–2000), Birla-3M India on March 15, 2001. Mr. Scheela's current position at 3M is Business Development Director, Transportation, Graphics & Safety Markets.

Background

3M's presence in India started in 1987–88 with a joint venture and one person on the ground. At that time, by law, it had to be a joint venture and foreign companies could not own more than 50 percent. In our joint venture, 3M owned 40 percent, the Ashok Birla group owned 40 percent, and 20 percent was in public shares. In 1991, we built a plant in Bangalore, finalized the investment from the partners, and sold 20 percent of the shares on the public market.

Since 1991, the equity has changed and the focus has shifted. Initially we focused on emerging infrastructure such as telecommunications and roads. Around 1993 additional funds were put in by 3M, changing the equity holding to 51 percent for 3M. In 1998, Yash Birla sold 25 percent of his shares back to 3M. Now 76 percent is 3M and I believe 8 percent is Birla Group and the remaining 16 percent is publicly traded.

In 1995, when I got to India, we developed an India plan that focused on 6 or 7 product areas. We were one of 3M's smallest subsidiaries and we had to decide which opportunities to go after with a small staff of about 120. 3M has something like 50,000 products and 40 different businesses. We focused on medical products, by selling tapes and dressings used in operating rooms to the largest private hospitals. In telecommunications, we manufacture a molding that makes tiny connectors which you use to clip two wires together. We also make more sophisticated boxes that have fiber products within and detection systems to help locate buried cables.

On the consumer side, there was Scotch Brite™, the cleaning pad. We decided to be first in that category, a non-woven category. Everything else was more industrial so with Scotch Brite, our intent was to go after the middle class consumer.

One thing that has changed over the last couple of years is automotive. Many new players have come into India. Automotive is a big opportunity for the things that 3M sells—various abrasives, sandpapers, graphics or decals for two-wheelers, and other consumer products within automotive. In the automotive aftermarket we sell different products, depending on the application. It might be dust masks for body shop workers or a different kind of sandpaper for body work. The key thing is to be in different channels.

One surprise for us was in the area of communications. We sold multimedia projectors that you would use to give a presentation. You hook your laptop into one of these and it shoots up all these nice fancy charts. These are very expensive units, but the market was unbelievable. The target market is multinational businesses along with institutions and governments. What really surprised us was the minister of Andhra Pradesh who wanted to have video conferencing with all of his offices in rural areas.

In India, 3M can sell small stuff like the Scotch Brite that sells for about ten cents, big stuff like projectors which sell for about US$1,200, and everything in between.

Political System

Certainly on paper the political system looks the same when you have a democracy with officials elected by the people. I guess here in the U.S., I look at the impact that highly educated voters have. Here you have discussion and debate. You want to know the platforms and the differences between Bush and Gore and between candidates at the State level as well. But in India, in the five years I was there, you never heard what anyone stood for. At the risk of being unkind, there it seemed to be election by the masses, based on what kind of gift they received from which candidate.

Familiarity with Free Enterprise

At 3M we relied on the locals to work with the government. However, we did use some consultants who could help us get in the door, to guide us with how to make the appointments, the correct protocol for letters, and so forth. We have actually moved a step forward and now we work with the government on various legislation such as environmental concerns and work conditions related to occupational health with respirators.

From a business standpoint, I would say Indians are very familiar with free enterprise. Maybe there are different attitudes toward equity. For example, we had our first sales contest where only about 10 percent are winners. That win-lose scenario was not always accepted by some people. They would expect to do their jobs and be left alone. So as we got more performance-based, I think some people were uneasy with that. I do not know if that was more of an Eastern philosophy or more individual based.

We started out small and people thought, to use a sales analogy, "If I could get to the point where I could have five accounts and am selling X amount that would be great." Well, in three years you are there and now you want to double sales. We did not always have people who had the burning desire, or what we would call "the fire in the belly" to raise the limit. Every year we were expecting more. We found people who were very good at that, but we also had people who did not want that bar to be raised.

Definition of Middle Class

In India, I would say it is a family with two kids, probably living with parents. They might live in a house or it might be an apartment, renting or owning. A few times people in their 30s would come in and say, "Here is my phone number." They just got their first telephone and that was a big deal in 1996. By the time I left in 2000, the same person might have a cell phone so another phone was no big deal. That was how fast that changed.

I noticed many changes even within a one-year time span with a significant increase in the goods available in stores. Companies like Sony are coming in and pricing specifically for the Indian market. By the time I left, Bangalore had at least 50 pizza places. The retail chains were also increasing.

Indians are very focused on their children and on education. They just want to get a good ranking in school.

Indians are very focused on their children and on education. They do not want to be bothered with sports. They just want to get a good ranking in school. My secretary would take vacation days to help her children study for a test.

Distribution System

There are no national distributors in India, so you are always starting from the beginning whenever you enter a new region.

For the most part, 3M uses distributors in India, but it depends on the industry. There may be a distributor who is already selling to a hospital, for example, who is willing to take on 3M products. By contrast, in the automotive area, we would be more likely to make a product on demand and deliver it to schedule.

The most challenging distribution for us was for Scotch Brite where we wanted to go right to the consumer in various stores. In a major city, there may be 20 or 25 market areas, with 15 or 16 stores in each one. We wanted to be in every store that sold pots and pans, cleaning products, and other household items and to find someone who distributed to all the markets in a city. No distributor existed so we had to set up our own distribution system in a sense. We had regional people in the major cities who monitored distribution and warehousing for us. Then an agency with dedicated sales staff would go to the market and sell cases of Scotch Brite to individual stores.

Distribution is usually labor intensive. There might be 200 people who would visit the six or seven stores in every market in every city that we try to reach. We rolled out our sales to large stores and then smaller ones. You have to figure out how to get to 5,000 stores, then 10,000, and it is a never-ending process.

There was no national anything. There was not a national trucking company or even national stores. India is a nation of millions of very small, mom-and-pop shops. What we were able to find was good, professional people, which is probably the strength of India. There are well-educated people with excellent business acumen who understand merchandising, business practices, marketing and so on. It was not easy to find the right kind of people, but not a huge challenge either.

Competitive Environment

There is such diversity in India in the economic spectrum, best practices, and all that sort of thing. There is centuries of technology, some leading edge and some that goes back thousands of years and you have to find that right niche. So at the same time we are selling the latest technology there, we might also find we are selling products that are being used as they would have been ten years ago.

For example, look at the mass market on metal finishing or woodworking, where people are still doing things by hand. They are concerned more about the price of a sheet of sandpaper, is it Rs 3 (US6¢) or is it Rs 5 (US10¢)? It doesn't matter that our Rs 9 (US20¢) product will last three times as long or make the work go five times faster with a machine, because they do not have a machine. On the other hand, you could go next door and find someone making engineered parts for jet engines, or whatever, and they would be state-of-the-art. They would want the latest and greatest innovations, and yet across the street you could not sell anything to another customer.

Of course, we ran into a lot of competition, but things were changing. The local manufacturers had to act quickly to upgrade their practices. The shiny car had to equal the shiny car of the Opel Astra. The domestic companies might do it differently, but they would certainly upgrade their systems to get there.

There was no national anything. There was not a national trucking company or even national stores.

Management Style

In general, the management style is authoritarian, almost militaristic. At the same time, however, you have the phenomenon in Bangalore with the software companies. They want to be Silicon Valley, and they were building the gymnasium and all the fun stuff that Microsoft had.

The banks are typical of the hierarchy. They are more nationalized, slow-paced, go and do your job, more unionized and so on. But then again there are world class companies like Hindustan Lever and Asian Paints, TVS, Suzuki, some real top-notch companies that employed similar programs and practices that we had. Our HR manager would sit down and counsel with various companies in Bangalore, and talk about localized programs for things like compensation packages, profit sharing, and stock options. Some of these best practices were shared by a certain number of the companies, but what was true at the top 10 or 20 companies was not being practiced by the bottom 50.

Marketing

I would say that marketing was one of our weaknesses. We were sales focused. As for positioning and marketing, that came later—like branding which also was just evolving. We had perhaps 8 or 10 marketers and 100 salespeople, whereas a typical 3M subsidiary would have 30 marketers. We relied a lot on our Asia Pacific people from Singapore who would come in and help us on the marketing side.

Getting market research in India is not a problem. You do not have to bring in experts to do that. We found a lot of local talent in this area. What we might do is bring in someone from one of our businesses who had been in Latin America or had gone through similar programs to help us interpret the data and say this is what this means. So we used 3M experts. Sometimes we had good surveys and bad surveys, just like anywhere else.

You can use segmentation. There is a wealth of data by social and economic class and purchasing habits. In retail, we would find that the retailers had no information. We tried to educate them. In the last couple years that I was there, there was a retail chain out of Chennai and Bangalore that could tell you exactly how many customers walked in there that day and the average purchase for each customer. Some retailers now have the power of information similar to what a Wal-Mart would have—very savvy people. This is probably the case for six or seven stores in each major city.

Advertising and Promotion

The promotional approaches in the U.S. and India really had to be different. One interesting thing in television: We started getting TV channels from Singapore into India and some companies would try to run an overall Asian commercial. Those were not always very successful. Sometimes you would see commercials by Bajaj, Maruti-Suzuki, and various consumer companies that were obviously focused on the Indian market itself. However, there was a world of difference in effectiveness, in the message, and everything else between the Pan-Asian commercials and the ones for India.

Just a simple example. The tag line for Scotch Brite pad is always "lasts longer." A customer in the United States might expect it to last two days longer. In India, consumers would expect it to last two months longer. If it does not last longer then they send it back and say, "This does not last longer. I have been using the plastic ball that I have been using for three years and I want my Rs 5 back!"

When you say things last longer, what does that mean? In India, we would tell people that using Scotch Brite would let them use less powder to clean the utensils. This saves you money. That was the promotional message with Scotch Brite in India. In the U.S. it is convenience, it is ease, how it can kill germs, but not in India. There it saves you powder. In India, we also would sell that product as singles. You might buy one or two. There are no multi-packs. The purchasing habit is not to buy something and store it at home. Rather people buy what they need today. It has to be small and inexpensive, under Rs 100—or about US$2.25.

The U.S. dollar was worth 48.66 Indian rupees on February 21, 2002.

Marketing Process

3M is organized into certain geographies, but ideas are exchanged among the groups. Everyone uses similar processes as far as research, studying consumer behavior, and brand differentiation.

Product Standardization

About 70 percent of our products are used straight out of the box. When you hook a projector up to a laptop, it has to work everywhere, whereas when we look at Scotch Brite, it may have to be localized for certain reasons. In the U.S., Scotch Brite is a laminate, a pad and sponge. When I was in India we could not sell that particular sponge because of restrictions on imports. That may have changed in January 2001. What we sell there is just the green pad, with no sponge attached to it on the other side. When I saw it first, I said, "Where is the rest of it," and they said, "No, this is what we sell."

On the industrial side, it depends on what market the product is being made for. If a refrigerator or motorcycle was being exported the manufacturer had to use all the good stuff. If it was staying within India, you had to match price-conscious competition. But as other competitors came in and raised the quality threshold, the difference narrowed between exports and products sold domestically. For a product like sandpaper for the automotive industry, we make it to the same specifications that we would in Detroit.

Cultural Differences

Teamwork in India was tough. Maybe this is an unfair example, but when you mention the top cricket players in the world, three or four are Indians. However, when you look at team results, it is very disappointing. So you end up with good individuals, lousy team.

It translates to business as well. You end up with the individual philosophy: "I stated my opinion; the team is going the other way and I object. I am not going to participate. I am going to separate from this team. I am going to make an example of this team because they are wrong and I am going to hold them back." Sometimes people would want to resign, but we might say, "I don't think so. You are on the team. Use your persuasive skills to get your point across." We might vote, or I might say, "We are going to do it this way. Knock that stuff off. Now we go into implementation. That is what a team does. It says we are going to take the ball and go forward." Initially we had people who didn't get that and we ended up doing some kind of organizational cohesiveness training. It was very tense and exciting to get people on a team going.

We did a survey in our company regarding the top five or six things that people liked at 3M. Some said innovation, leader in the industry, and rated number four or five was policies. The rules were clear and transparent. If we spelled out the rules for a sales contest and followed them precisely, people liked it.

Indians understand authority within the organization. For me it was almost embarrassing. If it seemed like a chair in a meeting was meant for me, it didn't matter if I sat somewhere else in the room, the chair would remain empty. Such reverence. I even tried changing the chairs and finally people caught on. And in our employee satisfaction committee meeting, I would say nothing, I would just let people talk. I might say how about this or do you understand this, but I would make no decisions, it was an open forum. It took three or four of these to really get it going, to knock down some of those barriers, but it eventually worked. It was real important to somehow send signals that we can talk and you can express your opinion, but it was initially like pulling teeth.

Gender Differences

I think the gap is narrowing, but women are still likely to leave their jobs when they get married and have children. When I went to more traditional companies—the automotive companies, for example—the engineers would all be men. I think in Detroit, there would be more women. Even when the company wants to upgrade a woman's job to a more professional one, some women will say, "No. I just want to be a secretary. That is my role."

Comparisons between India and China

For one thing India has been on a reform wave for about 10 years and China has been on it for about 20 years. So China is ahead of the curve on that. We may not like their human rights, but the fact is that in China there are a lot of people better off today than they were ten years ago. They have consuming power. They have better health care facilities, better education. People can fulfill their dreams better from what I understand. Whereas in India, there are still 400 to 500 million people who are still three centuries away from today. From my perspective, when the government came out with its budget I would look at whether they were going to reduce the import taxes. However, the important thing is to get people clean water, access to hospitals, and an education. The educational system leaves out a big chunk of the people at the lower end of the economic spectrum.

Projections and Challenges

When you look at the middle class in the last two years, there are certainly more choices available to consumers, an upgrade in the quality of life, and it seems to be accelerating. People in the middle class buy cars, motorcycles, consumer goods, and homes, and that feeds the rest of the economy.

There are still some major hurdles in figuring out the winners and losers and we have to see how that transpires. But India has got to be one of the mega-economies of the future. I do not know if it is going to take off. However, it does not have to be a tiger. There is nothing wrong with an elephant just moving ahead as long as it is moving in the right direction. Look at some of the other Asian countries who built real estate that was not on sound economic fundamentals, who goofed around with their currency rates, and made loans that did not make sense. That caught up with them. But if you go with solid economic growth, strong fundamentals, and continue to make the system work better, it is going to move along at a faster pace.

CHAPTER 2

Understanding India

INDIA is a complex mosaic of history, culture and politics that defies simple explanations. Paradoxically, this is a country where the old and the new seem to coexist with relative ease; a country that has a democratic tradition and a mixed economy, and where free market traditions coexist with the heavy visible hand of the government that has swathed the economy in red tape. Further, it is a country with nuclear capability, highly trained scientific talent, and at the same time, one of the highest poverty rates in the world. India is Janus-faced in many ways. On the cultural side, this is a country that is bound by the weight of traditions, religions, and cultures. On the business side, it has the entrepreneurial energy to drive it forward on a modern trajectory. The culture and tradition on the one hand condemn materialistic values as alien to the ascetic spiritual tradition of a country soaked in Gandhian values of non-violence and non-material interests. On the other hand, today the country has a burgeoning middle class that, particularly in the younger generation, is as materialistic as its counterpart in other consumer-based economies. So, which is the real India? Is there a way to understand this huge sub-continent in all its richness and complexity?

This is a country where the old and the new seem to coexist with relative ease.

The Western press is known for portraying India as having only one dimension. Poverty and squalor are underscored to the exclusion of the many achievements in science and technology. Of late however, this view of India as merely an economic backwater mired in poverty has been silently undergoing a sea change. Piquing the interest of foreign businesses, large and small, is the country's growing middle class with increasing levels of purchasing power. Foreign investors are also interested in India's information technology sector, which is growing by leaps and bounds. The government seems to have finally awakened to the possibility that this transformation could release millions of people in the country from their decades-long prison of poverty. In fact, it has started modifying its investment policies to be more hospitable to foreign investors. Unlike China, the government of India's timid moves have not opened the floodgates to foreign investment, but have piqued interest in the country. Today, we see Western investors gingerly testing the waters and contemplating investment in India's economy.

India today is a marketplace in transition.

India today is a marketplace in transition. This chapter offers a quick overview of the key milestones in India's economic and political history that precede the country's cautious move to a market-based economy. In order to understand the role of government, its love of bureaucracy, its tradition of a mixed economy, and its attitude toward wealth creation, we will discuss four key periods in India's history:

> British Era
>
> Post-colonial Era
>
> Pre-liberalization—1970s and 1980s and,
>
> Liberalization—1991 and beyond.

We then trace the country's development through these periods primarily in economic and political terms. The common thread linking these eras is the waxing and waning influence of the government on the economy.

British Era

Before 1947, India was a model colony, the crown jewel of Britain's colonial empire. For nearly two centuries, the country was a pawn in British empire-building plans, providing a ready source of raw materials to the mother country and serving as a captive market for her value-added goods. India provided the raw materials to power a sizeable portion of Britain's Industrial Revolution. The arrangement worked in Britain's favor, but served to suffocate India's economic growth by creating an economy heavily reliant on primary goods production and one that could not produce more sophisticated, value-added goods.

In order to facilitate their control of the sprawling sub-continent, the British created in India a cadre of civil servants composed of the educated Indians, who soon became rather adept at imposing a bureaucratic system on the local populace. The civil service created layers of hierarchy and bureaucratic rules to control the distant colony, but its side effect was to stifle free enterprise in the economy. The British also bestowed upon India a legal and educational system and sewed the sub-continent together with a vast railway network. English became the lingua franca of the legal and educational systems as a consequence of British rule. Having a common language was useful in tying together a sprawling country of diverse ethnic groups—a nation so unwieldy that Winston Churchill once declared, "India is no more a country than is the equator." Even today, in spite of India's attempt to reassert national pride by replacing English names with ones from the local languages, the English language offers India an advantage. Compared to China, India's educated, particularly scientific and technical communities are familiar with the English language and use it with ease. This is one reason why global multinationals today shop India for some of the world's most abundant and low-cost talent in software and information technology.

English became the lingua franca of the legal and educational systems as a consequence of British rule.

Politically, Britain's divide-and-rule policy kept tensions between Muslim and Hindu India at a simmering point, facilitating the continued British hold on the sub-continent. When the British left India in 1947, the country was partitioned into India and Pakistan, creating a separate homeland for the Muslims. Partition involved a great deal of bloodshed, dislocation, and Hindu-Muslim violence, which still mars the region today.

The net result of British rule on India had mixed consequences. On the positive side of the spectrum are the legal and educational systems inherited from the colonialists. The most negative outcome was the engendering of a national inferiority complex in the Indian psyche. This is reflected even today in the Indian love of foreign products and the perception that these products are superior in quality. Mahatma Gandhi, the leader and catalyst for independent India, was himself an initial product of British education. However, after his education, he went to South Africa. There, as a person of "color" he was rudely awakened to the inequities in that country and realized that his fellow countrymen suffered similarly under colonial rule, even if it was not called apartheid as it was in South Africa. He returned to India a changed man, infused with a near religious fervor to rid the country of an alien power that held the country's vast energy at ransom. He was willing to sacrifice all material goods for himself in order to bring attention to the need for self rule. The freedom movement gained momentum under a charismatic Gandhi and others such as Nehru, and in August 1947, an independent India was born out of the ashes of British India.

Post-colonial Era

The birth of independent India coincided with the hegemonic aspirations of the Soviet Union and the popularity of socialism and state planning. As the first prime minister of independent India, Nehru was quick to embrace Fabian socialism as the way to obtain economic growth for the new country. This choice was driven partly by a pragmatic belief that this was the best road to alleviating poverty and partly by a desire to shun all systems associated with the country's erstwhile rulers. The colonial experience led India's leaders to turn to economic self-sufficiency under autarkic socialism.

As *The Economist* pointed out in 1997,[1] Nehru wanted to attack two main evils of the colonial era, rural feudalism and the de-industrialization of India. Rural feudalism was the result of a polarized social and economic system which allowed the wealthy landowners and aristocrats to lay claim to a large share of the national income at the expense of the poor, who worked in near serfdom to the landed, moneyed class. The de-industrialization argument stems from the fact that before the Raj, India had a strong manufacturing sector. After colonization, India transferred capital to Britain at the rate of 1.5 percent of GDP annually throughout two centuries of colonial occupation. This led to the conclusion on Nehru's part that an export orientation for the new country would lead to nothing more than colonial exploitation.

Nehru believed in scientific and social progress and wished to modernize the country. He fervently believed that an omnipotent government had all the answers, and could cure all ills. This meant building and enlarging the inherited bureaucracy, albeit to suit Indian objectives. Following a policy of state control of the economy meant creating massive state-owned enterprises and putting the state in control of the commanding heights of the economy. A series of carefully crafted five-year plans charted the country's economic growth as orchestrated by the government. Unlike the East Asian model of state intervention, where government hand-picked private sector firms in key industries to support and nurture with state resources, the Nehruvian prescription sought to put the government in charge of the key sectors of the economy, particularly heavy industry as in the Soviet model. Competition and efficiency were not on the planner's minds, so the result was a labyrinthine set of controls on business and a licensing regime designed to ensure complete government control over production quantities, prices, and employment. Private firms were allowed to exist in this situation, but were bound by a plethora of ill-conceived rules and regulations aimed primarily at inhibiting economic growth. However, these rules also protected them from competition. Strict licensing requirements meant getting permission from the government to add capacity, produce a new line of product, and even to exit the industry when the firm was going under. The *license raj*[2] meant little or no competition between private firms, since the government would not allow too many players in the same industry in an effort to avoid what it called "wasteful duplication." The emphasis on developing the public sector at state expense and control created a system that completely lacked efficiency and accountability. The public sector undertakings (PSU) were unproductive white elephants that the state was burdened with feeding in perpetuity.

The "license raj" meant little or no competition between private firms.

During this period, state planning emphasized the development of heavy industry at the expense of agriculture. Protecting heavy industry also included imposing high barriers to trade and forsaking an export orientation to support its import substitution policies.

Nehru was a reformer with a zeal for education. However, his policies neglected primary education in favor of university or higher education. The irony of this emphasis is that today India is a country with one of the best pools of scientific talent in the world, while having a national literacy rate of a mere 52 percent.

The political alignment with the Soviet Union pitted India against the capitalist West, and clearly positioned it on the Soviet side of the ideological divide termed the Cold War. Given this ideological positioning, individual wealth creation was anathema and this seemed to fit in with the country's Gandhian predilection for spiritual, over material, comforts. The civil service inherited from the British served to stifle free enterprise in the economy. Efficiency criteria were overridden by perceived social equity criteria. The result was a gargantuan machinery of the state that ground on to the benefit of the planners and not to that of its citizens.

Pre-liberalization—1970s and 1980s

India in the 1970s was far behind the rest of the industrialized world on almost every indicator of development, from per capita GDP, to education, to infant mortality. Nehru's daughter Indira Gandhi, was elected prime minister in 1966 and saw fit to administer ever-increasing doses of the same medicine of government intervention to cure the country's economic ailments. Her brand of command socialism meant increasing government intervention allied with an increasing reach of the central government. Several key sectors of the economy termed pillar industries, such as banking and insurance, were nationalized and the public sector undertakings (PSU) comprised an increasing share of the economy.

Given her dictatorial approach to ruling the country, Mrs. Gandhi took the socialist agenda further by increasing price controls—implementing controls on trade and foreign investment that virtually sealed the economy and imposed heavy taxes on the rich. Foreign investment dried up quickly in such a closed environment, and the few high-profile investors like Coca-Cola left India under increasing pressure from the government to dilute its equity holdings and share technology as a condition of doing business. To Mrs. Gandhi's credit, the green revolution made India self-sufficient in food. Her other great achievement was winning the war with Pakistan in 1971. Her emphasis on agriculture was a reversal of the course set by her father, Jawaharlal Nehru, who neglected agriculture in favor of heavy industry. Agricultural subsidies by the government were meant to help the sector regain competitiveness, but as with most forms of government intervention, the key beneficiaries were large-scale farmers and not the smaller farmer. Even today, this sector has not been weaned off its subsidies and the difficulty of doing so is compounded by the political sensitivity of the sector. (Europe and the U.S., of course, have generally followed a program of heavy agricultural subsidization.)

During this period, India traded with the Soviet Union and its COMECON (Communist Economies, or Eastern Bloc) satellites, but had virtually no trade with the free-market West. Its home-grown industries were protected from harsh foreign competition by a series of trade and tariff regulations. Competition at home was controlled by a government that allowed only a limited number of firms in any one industry, in order again to prevent wasteful replication. In this environment, the producer was king and the consumer was left with little or no choice, in terms of product variety and quality. Also emphasized during this period were so-called small scale industries. Several product areas were reserved for this sector with the consequence that the sector could never attain the efficiency and scale to be competitive in an open economy.

Indira Gandhi lost the elections in 1977 and subsequently the Janata Party was in power for three years. She regained power in 1980 and was assassinated by Sikh military separatists in 1984. Her eldest son, Rajiv Gandhi was elected as prime minister that year and remained in power until his assassination by Tamil separatists in the state of Tamil Nadu in 1991. Rajiv Gandhi attempted to open the economy to foreign trade and investment, but his reformist intentions soon lost momentum in a cloud of alleged corruption scandals prior to his assassination.

Liberalization—1991 and beyond

The primary ideological impetus for liberalization was the collapse of the Soviet Union and the subsequent embrace of free-market philosophies by many former socialist or communist economies. A more immediate catalyst for economic liberalization for India was the July 1991 balance-of-payments crisis coupled with external shocks, such as the Gulf War, that led to an IMF conditionality loan. The economic crisis forced an unprecedented change of course from insularity to openness. Liberalizing the economy meant opening the country to foreign trade, cutting the size of government influence, privatizing a bloated public sector, and allowing the private sector more room for freer growth. Foreign capital and technology are the two main ingredients powering economic growth. In its efforts to integrate the country into the global system of trade, India has slowly but surely, started loosening or abolishing its myriad restrictions on foreign direct investment. Some of this has also been necessitated by the new world trade regime and India's joining the World Trade Organization (WTO). The outside world is no longer viewed as a threat, but as an area of opportunity. Economic liberalization has caught the interest of foreign investors who are venturing into India, albeit with relatively low initial investments.

India has slashed tariffs and made attempts to deal with the government budget deficit, but it has yet to deal effectively with the more painful and difficult part of the reforms. These include privatizing government enterprises, allowing imports of foreign consumer goods, and revising its rigid labor laws. State-run sectors such as telecommunications, banking, and air travel are being opened slowly to foreign competition and investment. The political ramifications of slashing payroll in these over-employed and inefficient sectors is a major hurdle to radical reform in these and other areas where the state has an ownership

The economic crisis forced an unprecedented change of course from insularity to openness.

stake. The government wants to see the states' role taper off gradually from economic activity. However, this implies an incremental approach that has bogged down by the democratic government's need to build consensus on economic reform.

In comparison with China, as noted elsewhere in this book, India continues to trail substantially in the area of Foreign Direct Investment (FDI), particularly in the manufacturing sector. Great hope is held out for exports in the software/services sector (see Chapter 14 on Information Technology). While there are ambitious targets for exports in the IT sector—as high as $50 billion by the year 2010—questions still remain. What is the likelihood that any economy, least of all one as large as India's, can grow to a middle-income level and significantly alleviate poverty without major investments in infrastructure and manufacturing? Still, at the beginning of the new millennium, considerable hope was expressed by observers both within and outside India that the economy will be able to grow annually at seven-to-eight percent and perhaps even faster as momentum picks up in the liberalization regime.

This sums up a brief view of India's economic and political history from the British colonial times to the present. For the potential business entrant from the U.S. or elsewhere, India's economy will continue to be an uncertain one that is subject to the shifting fortunes of coalition governments at both the federal (central) and state levels. However, there is also general agreement that the liberalization program will continue, and this should present major opportunities for the patient investor during the coming years.

NOTES

1. "India and Pakistan at 50: Happy anniversary?," *The Economist*, August 16, 1997, pp. 17-20.

2. "License raj" is a term commonly used in India to refer to the large private companies that held a "government imposed monopoly" and virtually served at the government's behest.

CHAPTER 3

Indian Politics

EVERY major developing market, including the Big Emerging Markets (BEMs), has its share of problems, and India is no exception. There are at least a dozen issues or concerns that any Western firm contemplating entering India should consider. This is especially true if the entry form is likely to be a direct investment. These issues are:

The Indian Central Government

The Indian States

Intellectual Property

Military Engagement

Infrastructure Concerns

Business Environment and Venture Capital

The WTO and Protectionism

Poverty

Role of Women

China

Bhopal

Education

While all of the above are not mutually exclusive, they will be considered separately. It is important to make certain that each is covered and given the appropriate perspective. Many relate to the Indian government, which is often led by coalitions and tends to be inconsistent regarding national priorities and critical development issues.

The Indian Central Government

The Indian central government is currently led by a rather loose coalition of parties (National Democratic Alliance) that have not really established a clear economic direction for the country. Part of the reason for this is that, like any coalition, there is internal disagreement on many key economic matters. Like the U.S. Congress, most major decisions are based on tradeoffs and compromises.

One concern is the strength of the government's resolve to continue to privatize the major sectors of the economy. To date, such moves have been slow and sometimes seem to take two steps forward and one back. Typically, privatization means major layoffs, as government-run businesses tend to become bloated with excess labor. Privatization in Central European countries, for example, contributed to rising unemployment. The same will occur in India, perhaps to an even greater extent. Whether the government can withstand pressures to slow down or further postpone privatization needs to be watched carefully.

The Indian governments of the Gandhi and Nehru era that followed British rule were strongly socialist. Therefore, there tends to be on-going support for public enterprises, even though many recognize the value of having a viable private sector that includes global MNCs. One must also recognize the influence of the giant family enterprises that have historically dominated the existing private sector. In the past, these enterprises have exploited positions of strength and to some extent they have operated under a protective umbrella of tariffs, quotas, and out-right bans of foreign products and investors. Anyone considering investing in India needs to carefully examine the country's current political situation and investment climate before making a decision. The trend today seems to be toward privatization and support for foreign direct investment, but the on-going shifts of parties making up the coalition and problems such as government corruption scandals tend to reduce the central government's power to take strong economic positions. A recent *Financial Times* article suggests that fighting within the coalition government distracted from the need to implement eco-

One concern is the strength of the government's resolve to continue to privatize the major sectors of the economy.

nomic change, while the bribe scandals exposed in March, 2001 have further weakened the coalition.

Let us cite an example. In March, 2001, Bangaru Lakshman, president of the ruling Bharatiya Janata Party (BJP), resigned in an arms procurement-related scandal.[1] (Apparently, Mr. Lakshman was videotaped accepting money to facilitate a military contract; a classic "sting" scenario.) This obviously weakened the BJP and reduced the power of India's Prime Minister, Atal Behari Vajpayee. Prime Ministers come and go, as with any democratic government, so the major issue is their ability to lead. Very often, the Indian Prime Minister is weakened due to the number of parties, the difficulty in reaching a consensus, or to a scandal.

As one U.S. MNC executive, whose firm has operations in India, stated in an interview for this book, ". . . there were four different governments that delayed any long term plans we had within India, because one thing businesses want is predictability and we were not getting that."

Firms need to be aware that the central government tends to move slowly and that economic change does not occur quickly. At the same time, the commitment to follow World Trade Organization (WTO) mandated reductions in tariffs, and other trade reforms seems to be strong and is opening the Indian market.

The Indian States

India has 25 states and seven union territories. The "wild card" in any discussion of the Indian central government is the power residing at the state level. The states vary widely in their power, influence, and willingness to move more quickly than the central government on economic development matters. In fact, some states have created an environment that is very attractive to Western businesses. The state of Karnataka, for example, has aggressively sought FDI and this has led Bangalore to become a leader in information technology. Many Western businesses base their operations in Karnataka. Clearly, these states

India has 25 states and seven union territories. The "wild card" in any discussion of the Indian central government is the power residing at the state level.

are making moves reminiscent of those made by U.S. states, such as Alabama and Kentucky, when they competed for foreign automaker investments. Bangalore, along with Hyderabad and Chennai, offers a highly trained workforce. Potential American investors in high tech fields should begin by looking at the individual states to determine what they have to offer in investment incentives. However, state powers are limited. The central government establishes economic parameters, such as the amount of equity that foreign firms and individuals can hold in business and regulations regarding such things as tariffs and intellectual property. Further, on occasion, the central government may need to bail out an over-zealous state. In the face of mounting pressures from the WTO, the Government did remove the protective quotas on some 1,400 products in 2000 and 2001.

Intellectual Property

Many of India's economic successes over recent years are tied to its failure to recognize the importance of intellectual property rights. For example, many Indian drug firms have copied patented drugs from the U.S. and Europe and sold them at prices far below global market prices. This lack of intellectual property protection resulted in many Western firms shying away from the Indian market or to their producing "second generation" products in the country. (Second generation products are those that are already being replaced by new products in the home market.)

Many of India's economic successes over recent years can be tied to its failure to recognize the importance of intellectual property rights.

Recently, due to threats from the WTO, India agreed to recognize pharmaceutical patents by 2005.[2] Some feel that a few high-end Indian pharmaceutical houses are capable of standing on their own, i.e. developing competitive original research that will lead to patentable products. It will be interesting to watch these developments, as well as those in the information technology (IT) area.

India needs to develop a history of insuring intellectual property protection to foreign firms if it is to achieve significant foreign investment in industries where such protection is critical. Similarly, it needs

Privatization Continues with VSNL

In February 2002, the Indian government completed the sale of stakes in VSNL (internet telecommunications services) and Indo-Burma Petroleum (gasoline stations). Further, the government indicated plans to sell nine companies by the end of 2002. The Tata Group purchased the 25 percent interest in VSNL, while the Indian Oil Corporation bought one-third of IndoBurma -Petroleum. The sales of both government businesses went smoothly, taking only six months to complete. The earlier sale of Balco (aluminum) took five years to complete. As this book went to press, Modern Foods (bread), CMC (software), HTL, ITDC, and HCI (hotels) and LJMC (mills) have all been privatized while several other government businesses, including Maruti (automobiles) are in line for privatization.

"VSNL Sales Gives Indian Privatisation Plans a Boost," *Financial Times*, February 15, 2002, p.19.

....

to address the problems of copying brand names and other copyright issues.

Military Engagement

In the February 26, 2001 issue of *India Today*, the editor stated that ". . . violence has the potential to tear the fabric of a nation, even one that has proven to be as resilient as India."[3] The editor cites terrorist problems in Kashmir and a number of militant groups in his analysis. Moreover, India has, of course, had ongoing problems with Pakistan that have led to a nuclear arms race.

To illustrate, the February 28, 2001 issue of the *Financial Times* reported that India had just tested a short-range surface-to-air missile. "The Missile is part of India's ambitious programs to build a missile arsenal ranging from nuclear capable ballistic missiles to short-range weapons."[4]

Surprisingly, while such problems involving great political risk have led the Indian government to use many of the nation's resources to maintain a strong military, they have not kept the country from moving forward. This has been especially true in states that are less directly affected by terrorist activity and not sharing borders with Pakistan, China, or Myanmar.

Such ongoing concerns, however, have resulted in India having a fairly high political risk assessment. For example, *World Trade* magazine had India rated 1 on a scale of 4 (safest) to 0 (riskiest) countries in its June 2001 issue.[5] As such, it was grouped with China, Kuwait, South Africa, and various Central and Eastern European countries. Among the countries ranked at the 0 level were Venezuela, Colombia, Vietnam and Turkey.

Infrastructure Concerns

For many Western firms, the primary concerns regarding India relate to its infrastructure. To fully develop its potential, India needs to make massive improvements in such infrastructure basics as telecommunications, electric power, and roadways. Some of these take time to correct. However, some states have taken measures to improve their infrastructures. One reason the Southeast area (Bangalore, Hyderabad, and Chennai) has been able to foster a strong IT industry is that it has taken a lead in some areas of infrastructure development.

India has a strong railway network. However, in a country so short on adequate roads, businesses that depend on motor transportation will find it difficult to establish a strong national distribution system. The lack of an adequate intra-city road system has made it difficult to establish a retail distribution system that could include stores of the caliber of Wal-Mart or Carrefour. Chain stores need to have the type of supply chain that is road-based. This is also a concern for consumer products.

Lack of electric power is probably the biggest concern. As Jack Welch, former GE CEO, stated in a speech in India in September 2000, "You don't have a chance to play in the 21st century without lots and lots more power." He indicated this is particularly true if the country is going to digitize.[6] The shortage of power and the continued rise in its cost take a long time to correct. The choice of an Indian site for an investment may well turn on this single concern. If the Western direct

In a country so short on adequate roads, businesses that depend on motor transportation will find it difficult to establish a strong national distribution system.

investor needs large amounts of electric energy in its production, it should raise this issue at the outset of its consideration of Indian entry.

Another major concern is the telephone/telecommunication limitations in the country. A major portion of the population, i.e. those residing in rural areas, does not have telephone access. India ranks among the countries with the lowest telephone densities in the world. The government has announced the end of its monopoly on long distance telephone service.[7] This move should not only increase service, but produce a drop in the price of telephone calls. Under the new plan, telecommunication companies that are successful in their long-distance telephone application will be required to service rural areas. They will also be required to give 15 percent of their revenue to the government.

Business Environment and Venture Capital

For many years, a relatively small number of large, family owned enterprises have dominated India's private sector. An excellent example is the Tata Group that has regularly been included among the world's largest organizations. The Group founded the biggest private sector steel company and is involved in truck manufacturing, tea production, chemicals, and hotels, to name only a few. With the increase in privatization, family groups such as Tata, are beginning to focus more on their main businesses.

Most of the U.S. MNCs operating in India that we interviewed were generally positive about some aspects of the country's business environment. They tend to be pleased with their joint venture partners, if they used this entry method. There also are few criticisms of the government per se. Rather, the slow pace of change and to some extent the socialistic orientation often frustrates them. They consider the Indian business community well trained and very business oriented. One U.S. MNC executive stated that one of the strengths of India is that it has very good professional people; ". . . well-educated people with excellent business acumen—understanding merchandising, business practices, marketing and so on . . ." Many see this as an indicator of the country's will to become a major international player. One test of the government's will may be played out in the way the privatization of Air India takes place. Air India and the domestic carrier, Indian Airlines, provide critical international and domestic service. Because of high losses in this sector, air travel has been high on the privatization list. Deregulation in the long distance industry seems to have dramatically improved service; hopefully, the domestic air travel sector will experience similar improvements as a result of privatization.

Despite some of the concerns noted above, venture capitalists continue to show a strong interest in India. Much of the funding has been directed toward the information technology industry. Prominent U.S.-based Indians have played a significant role in the investments, as have international funds, such as Intel Capital India, e-Ventures, and Chrysalis Capital. According to the *Financial Times*, in the first six months of 2000, 118 private equity deals worth $700 million were completed.[8] Subsequent dot-com/NASDAQ concerns in the U.S. did not appear to appreciably change venture capital interest in India. There is a view, in fact, that lower costs and high quality of India's IT sector will increase interest among U.S. and other foreign firms in outsourcing their work to India.

Venture capitalists continue to show a strong interest in India.

Nearly three-fourths of the venture-capital-fund deals in India in the first half of 2000 were in the IT sector, including both Internet and software deals. And, 75 to 100 startups ". . . have emerged with enhanced prospects of earnings and growth and a settled management . . ."[9] sufficient for second round investment. Most of these private equity deals involved international funds, such as Intel Capital India.

The WTO and Protectionism

Protectionism is deeply rooted in the government's psyche. For many years, it has benefited the large family industries and the large government-run, bureaucratic organizations. Protectionism has resulted in high prices for Indian consumers and arguably a lower standard of living. It has also become a major barrier to a modern, industrialized India. Change seems to be occurring, but slowly. Even as the country moved to meet WTO tariff reductions, it turned to quotas and similar measures to protect its indigenous producers.

Following WTO requirements in regard to sharply reducing trade barriers would undoubtedly result in the closing of a significant number of Indian companies and a consequent increase in unemployment. But there are strong incentives to comply. The WTO has taken action against the EU and the U.S. regarding their anti-dumping policies, and these actions have helped countries such as India. In fact, India brought a case before the WTO against the EU regarding its use of anti-dumping measures to limit the import of bed linen. The WTO's appellate body ruled in Spring 2001 that the EU's method of determining whether imports are being dumped was out of date. This provided evidence that WTO membership would have positive benefits for India, which has aspirations of being one of the leaders in the world body.

Poverty

One really cannot mention Indian politics and issues without mentioning the extreme poverty found in the country. There are many ironies found in analyzing the plight of the 250 to 300 million Indians who lack adequate food. At the top of the list would be the fact that government storehouses are filled with grain, much of which is likely to rot. Why? Because the government-owned food corporation provides an inflated minimum support price for wheat and rice production. Although the poor are entitled to buy this food at a discount, it is still beyond their means. Of course, waste and corruption further reduce what is available.[10]

A second government-related reason for poverty can be traced to socialist actions in the post-British era, which divided many large farms among the laborers. The result was many small (one acre or less) farms that are simply too inefficient and over-farmed to provide any real relief in rural areas where many of the poor and hungry reside. Finally, there is extensive corruption and many levels of management in the food distribution process, which siphon off food supplies directed to the poor.

Some hope appears to be on the horizon. For example, the growth of large-scale food retailers such as Foodworld, may lead to a better organized market for food producers. And, it has been suggested that the states be given control over food purchasing and management for the poor, which could be a marked improvement in some areas.

Role of Women.

One area where rapid change is occurring is in the role of women in the private sector. Women have long played a critical political leadership role in India. Indira Gandhi, for example, served at the highest level of Federal government, as the country's Prime Minister.

Only relatively recently, however, have women begun to fill senior management positions in both family and non-family Indian enterprises, as well as the MNCs. Of course, the very presence of these large MNCs in India has drawn women into senior management positions in increasing numbers, as has the rise in the knowledge-based economy. "With the accent on intellect rather than location, educated women have been filling top jobs not only in information-technology based companies and dot-coms, but also in financial service,"[11] according to an article in *Financial Times*.

Only relatively recently have women begun to fill senior management positions in both family and non-family Indian enterprises, as well as the MNCs.

China

As with its other border-sharing neighbors, India has historically had mixed relations with China. These have ranged from warfare to friendly trade relationships and everything in between. In fact, India's "socialist" era found the country having much in common with China and its other giant neighbor, Russia.

Today, China and India have moved closer to being market-based societies and each, along with Russia, welcomes trade with the West and encourages foreign direct investment. As members or potential members of the World Trade Organization, each sees the high potential of the others' economies. For example, Chinese enterprises have noted the large middle- and lower-income markets in India and are aggressively marketing there. As India reduced its import restrictions to conform to WTO guidelines, a number of Chinese firms have been

Trade between China and India accelerates

Trade between China and India has grown sharply in recent years. Moreover, both countries see the growth continuing in the future, even though it is still a fraction of each country's total global trade. China's Prime Minister Zhu Pongji's visit to India in early 2002 was designed to spur closer economic ties between the two countries. A problem, of course, lies in the low wage rates in China. However, China sees the potential for cooperation in several sectors and Mr. Zhu indicated that his country "could help Indian firms cut the cost of electronics through joint ventures." The Indian government is concerned about the trade deficit between the two countries, but China's entry into the WTO should mean its trading will be done within a rule-based system.

Source: Edna Fernandes, "India Faces Up to the Economic Flip-Side of China's WTO Entry," *Financial Times*, January 28, 2002, p. 3.

....

able to dramatically underprice the long-protected Indian producers. However, the two-way trade between the two giant trading partners has grown dramatically. Between January and September 1999 and the same period in 2000 alone, Chinese exports to India grew 32 percent and India's exports to China grew 60 percent.[12] China has at times dominated the import market for such goods as appliances, locks, fabrics, and toys to the point that the Indian government initiated anti-dumping investigations on several items. To illustrate, a 22-piece set of tools from China was selling for Rs 80, while its Indian equivalent was selling for Rs 400.[13]

What should be noted is that a number of Indian companies have invested in China or are outsourcing there. Pleasantime Products, for example, farms out its big orders to China while VIP Industries, a large luggage producer, is outsourcing in China, as well as producing locally. Rahul Bajaj of Bajaj Auto, a leader in motorbikes, says Indian companies pay more for power, capital, and wages than do Chinese businesses, ". . . which anyway hide their costs."[14] Clearly, India's years of government protectionism have fostered a business sector that finds it difficult now to cope with Chinese producers.

Looking beyond the current China-India trade picture, it is important to recognize that relations between the two countries appear to be warming. However, this could change at any time if one considers the past. The border dispute in Kashmir has not been resolved and two other Indian states (Sikkim and Arunachal Pradesh) are claimed by Beijing to be Chinese. Issues between the two persist regarding Tibet and other neighboring areas. Relations between India and China improved considerably following a visit by Li Peng, chairman of the Chinese National People's Congress, to India in January 2001 as well as Chinese Premiere Zhu Rongii's visit in January 2002.[15]

Nothing seems more deeply rooted in the Indian fabric than having a high-quality, higher education system.

Bhopal

One of the worst industrial accidents in history occurred at the Union Carbide plant at Bhopal, India in early December 1984. "Through 1996, more than 4,000 people have died as a result of the accident and 500,000 have become ill."[16] A tank at the plant leaked 5 tons of poisonous methyl isocyanate gas into the surrounding area. Among the resultant legal actions were a seizing of Union Carbide's Indian operations in 1992, charges of "culpable homicide" against the then CEO, and a $470M settlement in India's Supreme Court in 1989.[17]

While a number of years have passed since the disaster, it still remains on the minds of many Indians and Americans alike. A department of Bhopal Gas Tragedy Relief was established by the government and continues today, but the number of tragedy activists has sharply dropped in recent years.[18] Still, firms interested in operating in India need to be aware of the tragedy and the poor response made by Union Carbide to it. Dow Chemical acquired Union Carbide in 2001.

Education: Retaining Top Business and Technology Students

Nothing seems more deeply rooted in the Indian fabric than having a high-quality, higher education system. Thus, it is not surprising that Indians hold roughly one-half of all H1-B visas to work in the U.S., according to the U.S. Immigration-Naturalization Service. (H1-B visas are temporary work permits for skilled professionals.) In fact, about 50,000 Indian contract employees with H1-B visas work in Silicon Valley, which attests to the high quality scientific, engineering, and business training found in India.[19] (The number of Indian workers in Silicon Valley has decreased since the economic slowdown in the U.S. and the September 11, 2001 attacks.)

India's top colleges and institutes rank among the leading programs in the world, not just the developing world. Admission to these world class higher education programs is highly competitive; perhaps more so than most in the United States. Of course, a major concern for India is being able to retain a good share of the top graduates from the Indian schools, in order to stop the brain drain. According to the Chairman of the Aditya Birla group, the quality of the country's institutes of management and technology "has had multinationals scurrying to campuses to employ our finest young students."[20] In addition to the U.S., Germany, Japan, and Ireland have actively recruited in India.

India Today provides an annual ranking of the leading schools of higher education in India. Not surprisingly, the famous Indian Institutes of Technology (IIT) dominate rankings for the Engineering schools. The list for 2001 is headed by Indian Institutes of Technology, Kharagpur and includes the IITs in Kanpur, Chennai, Delhi, Mumbai, and Guwahati among its top ten.[21] Shri Ram College in Delhi, a school offering the B Com (Honors) degree, had the number one ranking among Commerce colleges. Its graduates and those of the other leading Commerce colleges provide graduates for high-profile MNCs and Indian firms.[22]

Another alternative for Indian students is the new "international standard" business school that involves a partnership with two well-known U.S. schools, Northwestern University and the University of Pennsylvania. The school, known as the Indian School of Business, is a project of several expatriate Indian business leaders, including Rajat Gupta, the top executive at McKinsey.[23] Located at Hyderabad, the school has "instant visibility" and features a one-year M.B.A. program.

India's top colleges and institutes rank among the leading programs in the world, not just the developing world.

Executives from several MNCs serve on the school's Board of Directors. The school should attract a continuous flow of outstanding students and faculty, another plus for direct investors operating in India.

The six Indian Institutes of Technology mentioned earlier were founded in the 1950s and were patterned after M.I.T. in the U.S. This led to the talent that produced India's IT sector, although many left for the U.S. and other developed countries. Today, there are many regional engineering colleges in India, as well as 30,000 computer-training centers. Still, there is an ongoing and growing need for trained IT people in the country. India is unique among developing markets in having produced such a highly skilled labor pool—one that has helped the West and still continues to drive the country toward a leadership role in the high-tech world[24]

NOTES

1. Gardner, David, "Bribes Exposé Sullies BJP Image," *Financial Times,* March 15, 2001, p. 4.

2. Shanker, Sitaraman and David Piling, "India Seeks a Cure for Tough Patent Laws," *Financial Times,* May 24, 2000, p. 12.

3. *India Today,* February 26, 2001.

4. "India Holds Missile Tests," *Financial Times,* February 28, 2001, p. 4.

5. "Political Risk Ranking Safest and Riskiest," *World Trade,* June 2001.

6. Gardner, David, "GE Chief warns India," *Financial Times,* September 8, 2000, p. 3.

7. Angus, Donald, "Telephony Shake-up to Put India's Villages in Touch," *Financial Times,* August 17, 2000, p. 3.

8. Merchant, Khozem, "India Continues to Attract Deal Makers," *Financial Times,* September 1, 2000, p. 22.

9. *Op. cit.,* p. 22.

10. "Grim Reapers," *The Economist: A Survey of India's Economy,* June 2, 2001, p. 14.

11. Merchant, Khozem, "A Handle on Power," *Financial Times,* September 6, 2000, p. 10.

12. Aiyar, V. Shankar and Rohet Saran, "Taste of China," *India Today International,* December 11, 2000, p. 28.

13. *Op. cit.,* p. 28.

14. "A Survey of India's Economy," *The Economist,* June 2, 2001, pp. 17, 20 and 21.

15. Gardner, David, "China, India Move to More Businesslike Ties," *Financial Times,* January 15, 2001, p. 2.

16. Czinokota, Michael R., Illka A. Ronkainen and Michael H. Moffett, *International Business,* Fifth Edition, The Dryden Press, 1999, p. 436.

17. "Union Carbide Corporation", *Hoover's 500: Profiles of America's Largest Business Enterprises,* Hoover Business Press, 1996, p. 485.

18. Pearl, Daniel, "An Indian city That Was Poisoned by Union Carbide Gas Forgets," *Wall Street Journal,* February 12, 2001, p. A-17.

19. Gardiner, Deborah, "Indian Expatriates Feel the Chill First in Silicon Valley," *Financial Times,* July 7/8, 2001, p. 3.

20. Birla, Kumar Mangalam, "Nurturing a Scarce Pool of Talent," *Financial Times,* June 15, 2000, p. 10.

21. Ghosh, Lobita, "Engineering: Top Ten Colleges of India," *India Today,* May 21, 2001, p. 17.

22. Goyal, Malini, "Commerce: Top Ten Colleges of India," *India Today,* May 21, 2001, p. 14.

23. Authers, John and Krishna Guha, "American Schools' Gifted Offspring," *Financial Times,* October 12, 1998, p. 12.

24. Creehan, Sean, "Brain Strain: India's IT Crises," *Harvard International Review,* Summer, p. 6.

CHAPTER 4
Cultural Considerations:
Impact on Business

CULTURAL collisions are nearly inevitable if one enters a foreign country without a clear sense of its values and belief systems. Bridging the culture gap is easier said than done. Even experienced global firms sometimes misread the hidden cultural codes of other countries and run into difficulties. The reason for the difficulty in interpreting the cultural message lies in the nature of culture itself, which in many cases is a complex amalgam of language, religion, tradition, and politics. The culture of a country is never transparent, yet it pervades almost every aspect of life and influences the choices of its people, whether in food, clothing, or cars. Culture also mediates business relationships, whether it is a relationship-intensive joint venture or a less intensive and low-involvement mode of doing business in the foreign environment, such as indirect exporting.

The culture of a country is never transparent, yet it pervades almost every aspect of life and influences the choices of its people.

   The other side of the problem originates from the "cultural blinders" which people from any given culture are prone to have. Consumers from a given culture think, feel, and respond in broadly similar ways.[1] In order for marketing communications to be effective, this psychic distance between the seller's culture and the buyer's culture needs to be minimized. Cultural conditioning, in many cases, mediates a manager's view of the world. James Lee calls this tendency to view one's own cultural standards as the norm and to measure other cultures against these standards as the self-reference criterion (SRC).[2] Managers operating in international environments have to view the world through multiple lenses—their own as well as that of the target market. This creates many opportunities for distortions in perception. Nowhere is this more common than in a big developing country, such as India. In fact, as we will see shortly, there are many cultures within India.

Demystifying India

India is not one monolithic culture, but a mosaic of many different cultures that, at times, co-exist in uneasy harmony.

The purpose of this section is to demystify some aspects of India's culture and to provide a business perspective on the cultural dimension in India. India's culture, like its history, defies simple explanations and broad categorizations. It is a vast and complex country characterized by a plurality of languages and religions. The U.S.-based multinational entrant, overwhelmed at first sight by India's exotic, even chaotic, sights and sounds, may be sensitive primarily to the differences between the West and this huge sub-continent. On further acquaintance, India's "liability of foreignness" is in many ways minimized by the striking similarities between the U.S. and India. Both India and the United States share a democratic political system, are familiar with free-enterprise, use English as the language of business, and have a cadre of technically trained talent. India has a sizable middle class, a portion of which is well-educated and has been exposed via travel to Western brands and products. What implications do these similarities and differences have for the western multinational marketer operating in India, or wishing to market to the growing millions of the country's middle class?

India is not one monolithic culture, but a mosaic of many different cultures that, at times, co-exist in uneasy harmony. The North and South are broadly divided by language groups. The urban and rural divide is one based on the economics of wealth and education. Furthermore, the caste system stratifies people by birth and creates disparities in consumer choices. Even the much-touted middle class is not a homogeneous entity, but is stratified by differences in purchasing power, which in turn are largely influenced by the urban-rural divide.

Several noted authors have provided explanations for the differences we note in people from various countries and cultures. For example, anthropologist Edward Hall contends that cultural programming influences a broad range of values associated with time, work, space, friendship, and business agreements. He further classifies countries into high versus low context based on their attitudes to these variables.[3] Vern Terpstra looks at values toward work, wealth and achievement, and acceptance or rejection of change, to develop a cultural frame of reference for a country.[4] James Lee uses the self-reference criterion to highlight ethnocentric behavior, which can misguide perception. Based on his study of IBM employees from 40 different countries, including India, Geert Hofstede identified four cultural dimensions—power distance, uncertainty avoidance, individualism/collectivism, and masculinity/femininity.[5] All these studies give us useful frameworks for understanding value systems that guide consumer choices and organizational behavior in the Indian context. They provide useful guidelines for understanding value differences when doing business in foreign countries, including India.

Sense of Time

In any culture, attitudes toward time are culturally conditioned and impact a wide range of business activities. A culture's attitude regarding time can be concrete or abstract, linear or circular. Business anthropologist Edward Hall calls this distinction monochronic versus polychronic time.

Monochronic time underpins most Western cultures and derives from the Industrial Revolution and the factory system, which tends to be mechanistic and future-oriented. Linear time can be quantified, controlled and parceled out in hours, minutes, seconds, and nano seconds. Time is a valuable commodity in this value system and needs to be used wisely, since it translates into money. Highly conscious of the tyranny of the clock, Westerners plan their schedules in minute detail to avoid any unintended waste of a commodity, which once lost cannot be recaptured. For example, a person waiting for a train in Zurich will complain to a stationmaster if the train is a minute late. Would someone from the U.S. react in a similar way?

This view of time can face some severe testing in a country like

India, which is largely steeped in a polychronic, elastic view of time, rooted in a centuries-old agrarian view. But, in today's India it is shaped by tradition as well other practical realities. Polychronic time is circular and iterative. The traditional Indian view of time is fluid and flexible; delays in keeping appointments do not carry the same meaning as in the monochronic West. A stated time for a business appointment is a rough approximation, and it is not necessarily construed as an insult to keep someone waiting. Furthermore, in today's India, the vagaries of public transportation, as well as the snarled traffic in most urban areas, create an element of unpredictability in keeping appointments to the minute. Religious fatalism deeply rooted in the Indian psyche could also be a contributing factor.

The traditional Indian view of time is fluid and flexible; delays in keeping appointments do not carry the same meaning as in the monochronic West.

This view of time has an impact on attitudes towards deadlines as well. In the West, a deadline, especially in the business context, is considered sacrosanct. One is expected to state clearly at the very beginning if one cannot meet a given deadline. This is not the case in India. The average Indian, in most cases, will nod acceptance to a stated deadline, but show no qualms about not respecting it. In fact, giving a very definite deadline to someone could be considered rather rude and insulting. Numerous stories of delayed shipments and unmet deadlines are an important reason why Western businesses hesitate to engage in business relationships with India-based firms, or outsource work to Indian suppliers. The Indian will in such cases lay the blame on an intermediary in the supply chain for the delay. One way to overcome these problems is to work with people with an established track record of on-time performance. James Lee explains this phenomenon of failure to keep promises in very plausible cultural terms. In his view, this trait is more common in cultures of low literacy, low economic development, and underdeveloped organizational systems. For instance, many business institutions in India, particularly smaller family-oriented enterprises, still operate on an interpersonal level and an important part of this system is to avoid open confrontation or disagreement on issues.

The rising TV food chef meets the multicultural foodie

Would you believe that on a busy weekend an estimated 80,000 pizzas are consumed in five Indian cities (Delhi, Chennai, Kolkata, Bangalore, and Mumbai)? This is a change from the tradition-rich cuisine that has long been a staple of the Indian consumer.

An India-wide food survey conducted in 2001 by McCann Erickson found that the country's middle class is rapidly expanding its food preferences. This new upscale consumer group is trying—and enjoying—new food tastes ranging from Chinese and Malaysian food to Mexican and Thai. Moreover, the middle income consumers in the major cities are eating out more and experimenting with all sorts of new cuisine, even at home.

There are many reasons, of course, for this new-found adventure in foods. Naturally, larger disposable incomes, more international travel, and the presence of global chefs on their cable TV screens have helped. Also there is a growing band of Indian executives—male and female—with 16-hour work schedules who find their time is valuable and that domestic help is at a premium. *India Today* even reports that Indian middle class consumers are becoming fans of U.S.-style TV dinners. Consistent with this interest in the new and often exotic foods is the growth in the sale of cookbooks and the reported 22,000 registered restaurants in India.

One additional result of this dramatic increase in food experimentation, especially with Western-style food, is the reinforcement of possibilities for the use of global marketing in India. This research highlights the growing influence of the country's enormous middle class and its potential for U.S. food-related items.

Source: Shuchi Sinha, "World on a Platter," *India Today,* Oct. 29, 2001, pp. 45–51.

....

As multinationals enter India in the post-liberalization era, they serve as agents of change in the culture. The sliver of educated, technically trained Indians working for multinationals and larger Indian firms who have to compete in other markets are forced to accept the Western view of time as a precious commodity. Many of the individuals in this segment of the population are educated in the West and return to India with a Western world view and time sense. These individuals should be able to gradually influence ways of doing business, along with attitudes toward time, in India. As the pace of life quickens in India's large cities, the traditional view of time will place a heavy burden on meeting the demands of a global marketplace.

High versus Low Context

Cultures operating on the monochronic time scale are generally considered low-context and those on polychronic time high-context. Low-context cultures tend to compartmentalize activities, contextual cues are minimal, and written agreements are heavily detailed. By contrast, high-context cultures rely far less on direct verbal and written communication, make more use of non-verbal and contextual cues, and may seal an agreement with nothing more than a handshake, since the context for the agreement has been painstakingly set by developing interpersonal relationships with the parties to the agreement. In high-context cultures, multi-tasking is a common phenomenon, where meetings are often interrupted, offices are relatively more open with much noise and interference. India falls somewhere in the middle of the continuum between high and low context. In the lower levels of the economic scale, business still revolves around interpersonal relationships, but business on a larger scale is conducted according to Western rules of contractual agreements. However, the power of the agreement is diluted by a legal system, which, though well-established in the British legal tradition, is slow to enforce contractual obligations. For the western businessperson accustomed to the habits of a low-context culture, operating in a high-context environment with its slower pace and numerous delays can be trying at best. An executive of a U.S. consumer-goods company operating in India commenting on the futility of trying to change the attitude to time, says, "You cannot force the Indian system, whether it is partners, customers, or government, to operate on your time scale." Changing one's own expectations of the pace of activity and adopting a longer time horizon may be the best strategy to achieve results in this context.

Individualistic-Collectivistic

Hofstede classifies cultures as individualistic or collectivistic. Individualistic cultures place value on individual self-expression and articulation of ideas, whereas collectivistic cultures communicate using culturally defined group norms. Power distance, another dimension identified by Hofstede, is a measure of the culture's attitude to inequalities of power and authority in organizations. The U.S. is low on power distance and high on individualism, as opposed to India which is high on power distance and relatively low on individualism. What implications do these differences have for marketing communications or advertising promotions? Kale argues the need for culture-specific marketing communications and uses Hofstede's framework to suggest more effective ways of marketing India to the American tourist. Since the two countries differ considerably along the dimensions of individualism and power distance, his recommendation is that the Indian Department of Tourism place particular emphasis on reducing the cultural distance between the countries. For example, tourist brochures targeted at the American traveler need to emphasize the "off-the-beaten-path" image, along with discovery and flexibility—qualities that highly individualistic American travelers find appealing. Power distance can be minimized by using informal, friendly communication, as opposed to the formal, rather stiff descriptive approach currently used in most brochures.[6] In terms of consumer product marketing, Samir Behl, vice president for international marketing, Pillsbury International, told us that in a highly individualistic country like the United States, a much greater variety of food products have to be marketed to suit diverse individual tastes. He adds that in a U.S. household with four people it is not uncommon to have four separate dishes, whereas in India, the family can do that in a restaurant, but not at home.

Uncertainty avoidance, the third dimension identified in Hofstede's research, refers to the degree to which people in a country prefer structured over unstructured situations. A society high in masculinity values assertiveness, performance, and competition, whereas a more feminine

The U.S. is low on power distance and high on individualism, as opposed to India which is high on power distance and relatively low on individualism.

society values quality of life, solidarity, and warm interpersonal relationships. India and the United States fall into the same cluster with
their configuration of masculinity and high uncertainty avoidance.[7]
Take, for example, the use of masculinity and uncertainty avoidance, as
considerations in the purchase of an automobile. One study shows
motives for buying automobiles in cultures clustered around the dimensions of masculinity and uncertainty avoidance. It concludes that people in these cultures tend to have a need for status, and have a
preference for powerful cars.[8] On issues defined by these dimensions
one could expect Indian and U.S. individuals to be quite similar.

Culturally defined motives can explain differences in sensitivity to
certain product attributes and advertising appeals. India is characterized by Hofstede as being a high power-distance, weak uncertainty-
avoidance, and a relatively group-oriented, collectivist culture, which is
high in masculinity. Hence, it may be more effective to present image-
based appeals that highlight positive social consequences. High uncer-
tainty-avoidance calls for communication that is explicit and directly
aimed at reducing perceived uncertainty and high power-distance
implies that expert advice from opinion leaders may be the most effective form of marketing communication.

Language of Space

Edward Hall, in his seminal study on the silent language of overseas
business, analyzes the use of space in different cultures to identify cultural signals inherent in this dimension. For instance, he points out that
whereas in America a spacious corner office signals status and power in
the organizational hierarchy, this is not necessarily the case in the Arab
world where there is no clear correlation between prime location and
power of the occupant. This holds true in India as well, though with the
recent entry of multinationals, the Indian view of space seems to be
changing.

Attitude toward Work

The Gandhian notion of work as noble and as an end in itself is not the prevalent view of work in India today. In the West, work is often a central theme in self-definition. One expects to meet not merely physical needs for shelter and security from work, but seeks to capture higher level benefits in terms of job satisfaction, growth, and self-actualization.

In an advanced industrialized economy it can be said that one lives to work. In India, where the pace of life is relatively slower and traditional values still predominate, one works to live. For an Indian, primary identity is based on family ties. Work and attendant material concerns come next. The value of work also differs sharply between the public and private sectors. In the public sector, which is typically overstaffed and where workers are assured of job security by politically powerful unions, work can be a charade. Workers in this sector often take inefficiency to new heights, and corruption is rampant in many situations. The state-owned Indian Airlines is a good case in point. Prior to liberalization, there was hardly any competition for the state-owned domestic carrier. Inefficiency in the form of delays and poor service were the norm, with little recourse for the flying public. Work, for the state employees, was a necessary and unpleasant evil, and the public experienced that insolence in every aspect of service that was, or was not, provided.

For an Indian, primary identity is based on family ties.

Today, as part of the liberalization program, domestic air routes have been gradually opened to competition from other domestic carriers in the private sector. The privatization move has had a noticeable impact on service and attitude to work in the State-owned airline. Feeling the sting of better-run competitors like Jet Airways, the state carrier has turned itself around in a remarkably short time to provide more competitive service. Even this new respect for diligence may be too late as the government has sought to sell the carrier to one of the major global airlines. Private-sector airlines train and motivate employees to provide good service and they work hard to keep to on-time scheduling. The attitude toward work in India's newly emergent private sector is closer to the Western attitude, in the sense that employees are well-compensated. In the case of service industries, employees receive incentives to provide good service. In other situations employees are motivated by the need to meet higher levels of service requirements as in the West. As key sectors of the economy are privatized and the country is opened to foreign competition, the attitude towards work is likely to change and perhaps even converge with Western standards.

Attitudes about wealth and achievement

Terpstra points out that a society's cultural systems of power, rank, and religion strongly influence its attitude toward the accumulation of wealth as well as its definition of achievement. India is a status conscious society. Rank is very visible and hierarchy is strong. In other words, power-distance is very high in Indian society, and subordinates are expected to defer to the wishes of those in superior positions in the organizational hierarchy. Team work in this context is not the norm. A deeply ingrained sense of hierarchy conditions subordinates to expect orders from above. The predominant religion, Hinduism, seems to sanction and reinforce this sense of hierarchy indirectly by stratifying people by birth into a system of upper and lower castes and numerous sub-divisions, all of which are strictly adhered to in most cases.

Mahatma Gandhi, in his struggle to restore equality to the downtrodden lower castes, sought to define religion in terms of non-violence and non-material lifestyles. One of the dimensions of Hinduism is its emphasis on transcending material life and the lure of materialism by detaching oneself from the desire for earthly possessions. This is seen as a necessary step for achieving "nirvana" by escaping the endless circle of life and death embedded in the Hindu notion of "reincarnation." In this view, wealth-creation is a drag on one's spiritual life. The process of seeking after it brings out the baser side of human nature and hence should be avoided. Work is considered good for the soul by Hindu philosophy, but the injunction remains that work ought to be carried out for it's own sake and not for the promise of material gain. In this process-oriented view of work there is still room for self-actualization and growth, but working for wealth is tainted by its material overtones. Pursuing wealth for its own sake will not only harm the spirit in this world,

In Indian society, subordinates are expected to defer to the wishes of those in superior positions in the organizational hierarchy. Team work is not the norm.

Who wants to be a millionaire? Indian-style

Did Indians react the same to the globally popular TV show as did viewers in some 30 countries and the U.S.? Despite the show's high market share and its dominance of its time slot, the *Financial Times* found that Indians view the show with considerable "awe and disdain." Moreover, the winners are not receiving $1m, but rather Rs 10m ($225,000). Why?

According to the report, "India's Brahmin-dominated caste system reserves little honor for wealth." In some ways, it seems to glorify poverty. Thus, a quiz show that drew spectacular audiences in the U.S. and elsewhere provides another perspective on the Indian "similarities" issue. It also provides a warning signal for those assuming few differences between the U.S. and India.

Source: David Gardner, "Indians face 10m rupee question: Do you sincerely want to be rich?," *Financial Times*, July 15/16, 2000, p. 24.

....

but significantly cut short one's chances of making it to the better part of the next. The popularity of the television show, *Who wants to be a Crorepati?* the Indian equivalent of *Who wants to be a Millionaire?* is a telling example (*Crorepati* means one who has ten million rupees). The show airs four nights a week and claims 40 percent of the television viewing audience. Yet neither producers, participants, nor spectators would admit that this show had anything to do with money! A study by Roper Starch Worldwide reported in the *Financial Times* found that contrary to the preference for money over time often found in global surveys, Indians said they prefer time over money.[9]

The growing popularity of amusement parks is another recent phenomenon in a country where the idea of a vacation for fun was not very prevalent. Ford has capitalized on this growing need for leisure and fun by targeting its successful marketing campaign for the recently launched Ford Ikon, at the "full of life" segment, which is motivated by a desire to work hard, play hard, and live a fun, aggressive lifestyle. In a similar vein, Samir Behl, vice president of international marketing,

The growing popularity of amusement parks is another recent phenomenon in a country where the idea of a vacation for fun was not very prevalent.

Pillsbury International, comments that the Indian middle class is no longer tied to the saving mentality, but is changing its attitude to one of living for the moment. As women enter the workforce, there is more discretionary income and there is a changing societal preference to spend money on items of self-indulgence. More money also equates to more emphasis on fun and on leisure activities. This translates to a greater need for convenience items. Mr. Behl adds that women still want to play a role in the family unit in India, and are hence more interested in ready-to-cook rather than ready-to-eat items. While saving preparation time, ready-to-cook items allow a woman to add her own condiments to the dish and serve it as her own.

The most popular actors and actresses in Bollywood films become cult figures.

For many decades, movie-going has been a popular way to spend free time in India. While a small section of the more affluent middle and upper income urban population does go to see Western (Hollywood) films, the vast majority of Indians go to see Indian produced films in both regional languages and in Hindi—the national language. These Hindi films originate mainly in the giant industry located in Mumbai (Bombay), which has come to be called *Bollywood*. The most popular actors and actresses in Bollywood films become cult figures who are frequently better recognized and revered than people from any other profession, including politicians and businesspeople. One famous actor who was the most popular hero in Hindi films throughout the last quarter of the 20th century, Amitabh Bachan, has gained a new following (just as his acting career was beginning to fade) in his role as the host of *Who wants to be a Crorepati?* For marketers, the power of the film industry, including the strong regional cinema industry in states such as Karnataka and Tamil Nadu, means that celebrities from the cinema world and music associated with films are the most recognizable spokespeople who can be incorporated in advertising and promotion.

Besides movies, the other great passion for a large cross section of the Indian population is cricket—a sport that is played all across the country. Like film-industry celebrities, major cricket players are easily recognized by the masses and have great potential as popular endorsers of products and services. Cricket matches between India and international teams can last one to several days, and both radio and TV audiences tend to increase greatly during the games. This, of course, creates good advertising venues.

Given the success of TV shows like *Who wants to be a Crorepati?* and the consumer goods examples, the view that wealth is bad does not appear to hold much currency in today's India, except perhaps with a small traditional, older segment of the population. As India integrates into the global economy, consumerism is on the rise and, firms local and international are vying to provide consumers a range of choices in consumer goods and services that did not exist before liberalization. This wave of rising consumerism coupled with a growing middle class that has increasing levels of purchasing power—fueled by increasing salary scales from global entrants into India—means a growing market for consumer discretionary and convenience goods. Branded goods are gaining popularity in India due to the implied quality guarantee inherent in a brand name. Indians are cost and quality conscious after having had to tolerate poor quality goods at high prices in the closed economic environment that existed before the WTO demands to drop trade barriers were put in place. As Walt Scheela, Managing Director, 3M India, put it, marketing the Scotch Brite scrubbing pad in India required a different positioning and marketing strategy. In the United States, the pad is marketed with the promotional message that it is convenient, lasts longer, and can kill germs. In the price and value conscious Indian market, the main selling point is that it is smaller in size and thus it economizes on washing powder usage.

Branded goods are gaining popularity in India due to the implied quality guarantee inherent in a brand name.

The Indian consumer today is exposed to new products and brands on a scale unmatched in history. In a country where the savings rate has been as high as 24 percent, families were motivated to save for an uncertain future. Most consumer goods were seen as frivolous expenditures. This view is changing now in favor of products that are durable with a good price-quality equation.

Rural India

Many of the changes that we have described in this chapter are most applicable to urban India. Generally, outside of the six major city areas that are discussed in Chapter 6, India remains a land of extremes that is changing ever so slowly. Rural India with its thousands of small villages and agricultural lands tends to be characterized by poverty and subsistence living. The gap between the very wealthy and the bulk of the population is daunting.

There are an estimated six million Indians residing outside India, and if they were a separate country, they would have a GDP of $25 billion.

However, again it is inappropriate to generalize. India's rail system, one of the biggest left by the British, provides a valuable linkage to various parts of the country. On the other hand, the Indian topography and weather have dramatically affected life in India. Annual monsoons cause extreme flooding and the rainy season can have a crippling impact on populations struggling just to get by. Similarly, the Gujarat earthquake proved a major drain on the country's assistance resources, as did the drought in Central India in 2000. All this offers little hope for the estimated 300 million Indians who exist on $1 per day. Clearly, the poor and the illiterate ". . . have little clout in India's democracy," as David Gardner wrote in a *Financial Times* article in February 2001.

The Third Face of India

One would be remiss in discussing the impact of cultural considerations on doing business in India without noting the role played by Non-Resident Indians (NRI) on the culture of the country. There are an estimated six million Indians residing outside India, and if they were a separate country, they would have a GDP of $25 billion. Many, of course, reside in the U.S., are U.S. citizens, and have been extremely successful. Their link to this chapter lies in the fact that a large share are in continuing contact with their Indian relatives, who also visit them quite often. Further, the NRIs often visit India and keep their relatives and family friends acquainted with the latest in U.S. products and services. Often, in fact, they return to India bringing an array of Western products.

While there are many other recent U.S. immigrants that have ties to their native countries, there are several critical differences in the relationship of the NRIs to India. First, their families in India often speak English and therefore, U.S. publications carrying the latest in fashion and business news can be understood there. Second, India has a number of outstanding business schools and many of their faculty members were educated in the U.S. and are familiar with U.S. business practices. Further, many leading U.S. business-school faculty are NRIs, and they frequently visit these outstanding Indian schools, thus providing a special link to U.S. business activity. Many of the latest in business approaches, techniques, and even cases are familiar to Indian business-school graduates. NRIs help many Indians of all ages to be up-to-date on U.S. brand names and marketing techniques. This is one reason many consumer and business-to-business companies use standardized promotion programs in India. Reinforcing the connection is the popularity of publications, such as *India Today,* both in India and among NRIs in North America. The popular weekly magazine even has a special North American section and can be found in urban areas throughout the U.S.

How strong is the connection to and familiarity with North America?

A giant political billboard advertisement in Chennai states, "Men are from Mars, Women are just down to Earth." This advertisement for female political candidate, Jayalalitha, uses a play on words from the well-known U.S. book, *Men Are from Mars, Women Are from Venus.* The political party would not have used such a billboard advertisement unless the voters in general were quite familiar with this U.S. title. The implications of this level of familiarity with so many aspects of U.S. lifestyles and consumer products should be considered by potential entrants into India.

NOTES

1. Hong, J.W., Muderrisoglu, A.M. and Zinkhan, G.M. "Cultural Differences

and Advertising Expansion: A Comparative Content Analysis of Japanese and US Magazine Advertising," *Journal of Advertising Research,* 1987, 16 (1), 55-62.

2. Lee, James A., "Cultural Analysis in Overseas Operations," *Harvard Business Review,* March-April 1966, 106-114.

3. Hall, Edward T., *The Silent Language,* New York: Doubleday, 1959.

4. Terpstra, Vern and Kenneth David, *The Cultural Environment of International Business,* Third Ed., Cincinnati: South-Western Publishing Company, 1991.

5. Hofstede, Geert, *Culture's Consequences: International Differences in Work-Related Values.* Newbury Park, CA: Sage Publications, 1980.

6. Kale, Sudhir H. "Culture-Specific Marketing Communications: An Analytic Approach," *International Marketing Review,* 1991, 8 (2), 18-30.

7. Zandpour, Fred and Katrin R. Harich "Think and Feel Country Clusters: A New Approach to International Advertising Standardization," *International Journal of Advertising,* 1996, 15, 325-344.

8. de Mooij, Marieke. *Global Marketing and Advertising: Understanding Cultural Paradoxes.* Newbury Park, CA: Sage Publications, 1997.

9. Gardner, David, "Who wants to be a millionaire? Indian-style," *Financial Times,* July 15.16, 2000, p. 24.

CHAPTER 5

Evaluating the Indian Economy

AS WITH many rapidly emerging markets, it is difficult to get a clear picture of the Indian economy. By some measures, the country has made rapid improvements over the past decade. It also has taken several critical political steps that are essential to achieving a leadership role among the Big Emerging Markets (BEMs)

India is a democracy and this can lead to slow response to change.

At the same time, there are a number of economic measures that suggest that India is failing to maximize its potential and that place it well behind China in the race for such a lead position. Frankly, one of India's problems is that it is constantly being compared with China. Both have huge populations and cover extremely large geographic areas. However, in many ways, that is where the comparisons should end.

India is a democracy and this can lead to slow response to change. For example, most business leaders and economists in the U.S. supported NAFTA and now support the Free Trade Agreement of the Americas (FTAA). However, we have seen how difficult it is to get the U.S. Congress and the public to support such a move. In contrast, China's government is run by a small Communist hierarchy and economic and political change can occur quickly. Thus, it is unfair to compare India's speed with China's in making their needed moves toward becoming a major player in the global economy. Yet such comparisons will continue in the business press. Our assessment of the country's economy and its potential for near-term change is, however, tempered by the political realities.

In this chapter, we will consider:

India's economic *pulse,* i.e. its situation in terms of traditional measures such as its Gross Domestic Product (GDP) and Balance of Trade.

India's areas of economic *strength* and its business/service sector development; and

India's key economic *concerns* and its near-term potential for solving them.

India's Economic Pulse

In 2001, India's GDP totaled just under US$500 billion, which represented a 6.6 percent rate of growth.[1] While this GDP total was roughly one-half that of China, it does represent a rather steady growth rate. What tends to offset the enthusiasm for this upward pattern is the rate of deficit spending by the national government and the individual state governments.

According to the U.S. Department of Commerce, industrial production grew 8.2 percent in fiscal year 1999–2000, while agriculture production declined by 3 percent over the same period. Agriculture, still the primary sector in India, accounts for 26.5 percent of GDP, and employs 62 percent of the workforce. Foreign direct investment totaled US$3.7 billion, which is quite small when you consider that the Czech Republic's inward direct investment totaled US$4.6 billion in 2000.[2] However, it is not surprising considering the slow rate of privatization in India and the bureaucratic and legal issues that still need to be resolved for foreign investors.

At the heart of current and future foreign direct investment expansion in the country will be the government's degree of commitment to privatization. A term that business visitors to India often hear (and read about) is *license raj,* mentioned in Chapter 2. *License raj* is best described as a concession awarded to an Indian company, often a family company like Birla or Tata. These licenses gave the company exclusive rights to manufacture certain products and provided high tariff protection. However, the licenses often forbade them from producing new products, diversifying into different lines, or investing or selling overseas.[3] There was little incentive for new and improved products, and limits were often set in production. After the license raj was abolished in the early 1990s, the Indian automotive industry grew from three firms making 190,000 old-fashioned vehicles to ten firms producing 500,000 modern vehicles.

As India completes its tariff reductions and reduces barriers to imports in order to conform to the WTO guidelines, some further increase in trade deficits might be expected. Oil imports alone grew by 64 percent in 1999–2000, but exports from the IT and other sectors. helped to partially offset this.[4] Further, imports from China of low-cost manufactured goods have led to selective use of quotas by the Indian government. It will be difficult for Indian manufacturing firms to continue to compete with China in several categories. This has led some Indian firms to outsource production or to set up their own manufacturing operations in China.

FIGURE 5.1 KEY ECONOMIC DATA FOR THE INDIAN ECONOMY

The government's annual budget for 2000–2001 was targeted at a fiscal deficit of 5.1 percent of GDP.

	2000	1999	1998
Total GDP (US$ billion)	$475	438	431
GDP per capita (US$)	$474	445	444
Industrial production (annual change in percent)	7.1%	8.2	4.0
Exports (US$ billion)	$43	37	34
Imports (US$ billion)	$53	47	45
Foreign Direct Investment (US$)	Not available	$3.7 billion	1.7

Sources: Financial Times, International Monetary Fund, U.S. Department of Commerce

FIGURE 5.2 INDIA'S MAIN TRADING PARTNERS, 1999 (IN PERCENT OF TRADE)

Trading partner	Imports	Exports
United States	9%	24%
Japan	6	5.6
Singapore	6	NA
Germany	NA	5.6
United Kingdom	NA	6

Sources: Financial Times, International Monetary Fund, U.S. Department of Commerce

U.S. INVESTMENT IN
INDIA, 2000
*Estimated Book
Value 10$ billion*

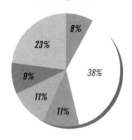

Fuel &
oil refinery	38%
Food processing	11
Telecom	11
Services	9
Elec. Equip.	23
Others	8

World Trade Market Focus

The June 2001 issue of *World Trade* magazine offered a good overview of what it calls India's pulse rate. The following comments and statistics on India are excerpted from that publication:[5]

Currency	Indian rupee
Exchange rate	46.58/US$1
Annual change	6.7%
Stock market change 2000–2001	-26.7%
Main imports	Crude oil & petroleum products, machinery, gems, fertilizer, chemicals
Main exports	Textile goods, gems & jewelry, engineering goods, chemicals, leather
Usual payment terms	60–90 days
Payment delays	1–3 months; letter of credit is recommended
Inflation rate (annual)	
2000 estimated	6%
2001 forecast	5%
GDP growth (annual)	
2000 estimated	5.8%
2001 forecast	6.0%
World Trade view	Domestic market still a question, but trade reforms and trade reductions for U.S. firms offer opportunities for outsourcing

Source: World Trade Magazine, June 2001.

Areas of Economic Strength

India has a vibrant information technology (IT) sector with a number of world class businesses. (See Chapter 14) Prior to the growth of the IT sector, the country was known for its successes in agriculture, the diamond trade, textile production, and clothing manufacturing. India has become a leading producer of wheat and rye largely as a result of its green revolution. At US$ 6 billion annually, the diamond trade is the country's largest export earner, much of it controlled by Palanpuri Jains from Gujarat. And, of course, India has played a key role in the textile industry for many years.

As previously noted, India's biggest asset is a large workforce that is well trained in the technology and science areas. It should not be surprising that India has a well-developed pharmaceutical industry—one that for years was known for producing copies of leading research-based Western firms' drugs. However, as intellectual property protection increases, several firms are shifting their focus to basic research, and indicating that they will be active players in the global pharmaceutical market of the future.

Interestingly, the *Financial Times* announced in its 2001 report of the world's largest companies that nine Indian companies rank among the "Top 100 Asia-Pacific companies."[6] When one considers

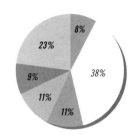

U.S. IMPORTS TO INDIA, 2000 *US$3.63 billion*

Machinery & transportation equipment	45%
Chemicals	24
Misc. manufactures	12
Manufactured materials	10
Others	9

FIGURE 5.3 SELECTED INDIAN FIRMS INCLUDED ON THE *FINANCIAL TIMES* LIST OF TOP 100 ASIAN-PACIFIC COMPANIES AND THEIR 2001 RANKING

Company	Market Capital (in US$ billion)	Ranking[6]
WIPRO	$13.0	21
Hindustan Lever	9.8	27
Infosys Tech	8.3	36
Reliance Ind.	7.2	42
Reliance Petroleum	5.4	52
IFCI	5.0	60
ITC	4.8	64
Oil & Natural Gas	4.0	75
HCL Tech.	3.4	90

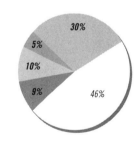

U.S. IMPORTS FROM INDIA, 2000 *US$8.54 billion*

Machinery & transportation equipment	5%
Food & livestock	30
Misc. manufactures	46
Manufactured materials	9
Others	10

"Star" for sale in public sector approach to turnaround

SIL or Scooters India Limited has been described by *India Today International* as an example of the Indian Government's version of a turnaround company. In order to make this public-sector three-wheel producer attractive for a private-sector takeover, the government wrote off Rs 609.77Cr in loans and interest.

With this sharp reduction in debt, SIL became ripe for privatization and government. The Ministry of Heavy Industry offered roughly three-fourths of the firm for sale. Not surprisingly, two private sector firms, Italy's Piaggio and Japan's Suzuki, were among those reported interested in SIL.

SIL offers a prime example of how a long poor-performing public sector enterprise can eventually become profitable. Without the removal of its heavy debt burden of loans and interest and a 1990's decision to move from a two-wheel to a three-wheel builder, SIL would have continued as one of many "un-privatizable" government properties. However, some 15,400 of the firm's seven-passenger three-wheelers were produced in 2000 and the future seems bright for SIL.

Source: Sumit Mitre, "Window Dressing," *India Today International,* November 13, 2000, p. 25.

....

that this list includes all of the major Asian countries except Japan, this number is fairly impressive. However, only WIPRO, a major software group that is featured later in this book made the FT500 (global). Also, it should be noted that these are publicly held firms and some partially government-owned (the list excludes privately held groups).

Another strength is the general improvement in the incomes and the quality of life for the lower-middle and middle-income groups that comprise roughly 60 percent of the population. In its February 19, 2001 issue, *India Today International* reported the results of a survey conducted in New Dehli, Bangalore, Kolkata (Calcutta), Chennai (Madras), and Mumbai (Bombay). Essentially, it asked a sample of the middle-income populations in these five cities how their lives today (2000) were different from ten years earlier (1990). In the five cities, 7 percent said that they had greater "earning power." More had color televisions and refrigerators at the top of their shopping lists. In 1990, electric irons were the favored items on their shopping list. But, most importantly, 83 percent felt that the 2000–2010 decade would be better than 1990–2000. This reflects an optimism that is essential for further economic development.[7]

What is currently in place is a viable business economy. The government has begun to direct its attention to privatizing major portions of the economy. The process has been unusually slow due to resistance from myriad government workers who recognize that true privatization would result in massive layoffs in some sectors. The country has taken faltering steps to privatize the airlines and banks. However, since the government is run by a coalition of parties aligned to produce a majority, it is doubtful many of the tough privatization decisions will be made in the near term. Still, it appears that momentum is building for gradually permitting a potent private sector to develop. Improved regulations for Foreign Direct Investment now make it easier to form a joint venture with the majority equity held by the foreign partner and to establish a wholly owned subsidiary. Certainly, the days of the *license raj* are at an end. Moreover, tariffs, a concern when a firm needs to bring in equipment, have been sharply reduced.

However, economic problems do remain.

Degree of Difficulty in Doing Business

In 1998, the World Bank initiated a survey in India as part of its larger 100-country study of the World Business Environment. The Confederation of Indian Industry conducted the Indian portion of the study. There were 210 business firms selected from across the country included in the study and care was taken to have good geographic representation. The study included a number of potential problem areas, such as the legal environment, quality and integrity of public services, and the availability of information on laws and regulations. It offers a useful assessment of conditions for operating and growing a business in India.

Many of the areas covered by the study are especially important to firms considering entering India.

Many of the findings in the study were not surprising and simply confirmed points made in other sections of this book. While the report is extensive, we selectively highlight a few of the findings.[8]

Legal/Tax Services

The majority of the businesses rated the quality of the judiciary/courts, customs, and tax (excise, income and state sales) services relatively highly. Depending on the service, 13 to 25 percent of the respondents gave a low rating. However, a clear majority of the respondents felt both the central government and the local and regional governments were helpful, a higher share than three years earlier.

Business respondents are generally optimistic about the future.

One concern that should be noted, however, is the confidence of the business community that the legal system would "uphold my contract and property rights in business disputes." Nearly 17 percent lacked such confidence. Further, most felt the legal system was not usually quick or affordable. Moreover, about one-third doubted its honesty.

Regarding the corruption of government officials, roughly one-half of the businesses indicated that it is common to make irregular additional payments to get things done. This is more common for smaller firms than larger companies. Unofficial payments were commonly made for electricity or telephone connections, licenses and permits, customs, and government contracts.

Despite the concerns, the business respondents were generally optimistic about the future. Two-thirds indicated their exports were likely to increase during the following year (1999) and 60 percent indicated they would be increasing their investments. The overall responses regarding the legal system, public services, and other issues are not unusual for an economy in the process of privatization, adapting to WTO, and other traumatic business-related changes. However, the issues raised should be considered by investors and become a part of their entry negotiations.

India's Key Economic Issues

Like most newly emerging economies, India has its share of economic problems and concerns. Over the past few years, the government has had a series of budget deficits, which naturally constrain its ability to solve problems such as poverty and lack of infrastructure. For example, while the government has grain elevators filled beyond capacity and grain rotting due to overproduction brought on by agriculture subsidies, it is unable to match the food with its poverty stricken population. Unlike China, which mandated one-child households to control its population to a manageable level, India has not had this option. In fact, poor rural families tend to have very large families. So there appears to be no near-term solution to poverty in most of the Indian states.

It appears that momentum is building for gradually permitting a potent private sector to develop.

India is likely to have severe Balance of Trade worries over the near term. Especially probable are large trade deficits with China. When you combine India's WTO compliance with tariff reductions, its higher labor costs, and less efficient producers in a number of sectors, imports from China and other lower cost countries can rapidly create major trade deficits. As mentioned earlier, some Indian companies are even outsourcing or setting up production in China in order to better compete with Chinese manufacturers. To offset some of these concerns, the Indian government has resorted to quotas, temporary tariffs, and so forth.

Another major economic issue in India is tied to its many infrastructure problems. This has been widely discussed in the business press and is a major concern for several U.S. firms we interviewed for this book. Time and again, there are concerns voiced about the power sector, the terrible condition of the roads, the port problems, and the telephone system. While there were two sides to the Enron case in India, (the now-bankrupt U.S. company built a major power facility and then found it unprofitable to continue there) the result is likely to make it difficult to rely on the private sector for energy solutions. And, in general, the utilities sector tends to be weak, although wireless phones have led to better access in remote areas and helped to improve communications. In our conversations with more than 20 major U.S. companies regarding their Indian investments, an on-going theme was how the poor quality of the Indian road system has hampered distribution and made many areas off limits to them.

In summary, there is much work to do on the country's infrastructure at a time when India is faced with the budget deficits and with little likelihood of doing a better job of tax collection or finding new revenue sources. The best hope is for privatization, thus reducing the size of government and the country's deficits. But again, taking such unpopular actions is difficult for coalition governments. This is especially true when the slim margin of leadership can be toppled by constant corruption scandals. An additional major expenditure for this emerging market is its military preparedness and actual on-going conflicts. These costs further hamper the country's efforts to solve poverty and infrastructure concerns.

NOTES

1. *The World in 2001*, The Economist Group, pp. 86–87.

2. U.S. and Foreign Commercial Service and U.S. Department of State, 2000, "Country Commercial Guide: India 2001".

3. Furman, Peter with Michael Schuman, "Now We are Our Own Masters," *Forbes,* May 23, 1994, p. 128.

4. Unger, Brooke, "The Plot Thickens," *The Economist: A Survey of India's Economy,* June 2, 2001, p. 2.

5. *World Trade*, June 2001, pp. 26–27.

6. *Financial Times*, "The World's Largest Companies," May 11, 2001, p. 53.

7. Bhandare, Namita, "Better Off Than Dad," *India Today International*, February 19, 2001, pp. 37-40.

8. *Survey of the Indian Business Environment*, Confederation of Indian Industry, April 19, 1999. A report submitted to the World Bank as part of its The World Business Environment Study "Measuring Conditions for Business Operations and Growth."

CHAPTER 6

India's Cities Are the Place to Start

INDIA has three entries among the world's 30 largest cities, according to the United Nations. The UN's projections add Hyderabad to the list by 2005. In this section we will describe briefly six major metropolises—Bangalore, Mumbai (Bombay), Kolkata (Calcutta), Delhi, Hyderabad, and Chennai (Madras). The names in parentheses are the Anglicized names used during British colonial times. The new names have been adopted to replace the Anglicized names. Of these six cities, all but two (Bangalore and Hyderabad) usually were recognized as the four largest cities at the time of Indian independence in 1947. Mumbai, Kolkata, and Delhi are among the 15 largest cities in the world. Bangalore and Hyderabad are two southern cities that have attracted great attention as the centers for information technology (see Chapter 14) during the past decade. These two cities were also the capitals of two of the largest kingdoms (princely states) during British times.

Any discussion of urban India must first take note of the large divide that exists between urban and rural areas on the one hand and on the other, between the urban poor and urban affluent within the cities.

Any discussion of urban India must first take note of the large divide that exists between urban and rural areas on the one hand and on the other, between the urban poor and urban affluent within the cities. Unlike some other regions of the world, (i.e. Latin America) India is still much more rural than urban, although with development it is experiencing the inevitable migration from rural to urban areas. Overall, though, less than 50 percent of India's population can be classified as urban. In the next few years, growth in the urban population is expected to keep pace with the projected economic growth of 6 to 7 percent. Urban population growth has contributed to a substantial increase in urban poverty. However, in the past decade since the economy was deregulated, there has also been a considerable increase of affluence among the urban middle and upper classes. This more confident and growing urban middle class has changed consumption trends for urban households and created new opportunities for products and services.

Profiles of the Six Cities

Bangalore

This city is called the "Silicon Plateau" of India. Located on a plateau more than 3,000 feet above sea level, it is the city that has been associated with the country's information technology industry. Because of its altitude, Bangalore enjoys mild weather for most of the year and is an attractive place to live. Over the years, it has drawn business people and investors from all over the country and today is home to nearly 7 million people.

Bangalore now has major centers set up by many leading IT companies from the U.S. and elsewhere.

After the deregulation of the Indian economy, interest in India's software industry increased. Bangalore now has major centers set up by many leading IT companies from the U.S. and elsewhere. Texas Instruments, General Electric, and Digital are three of these firms. It is also home to two of India's leading domestic software giants. One is Infosys, the first Indian firm to trade its global depository receipts on the NASDAQ exchange. It derives more than two-thirds of its annual revenues from operations in the United States. The other is WIPRO, which began as a family owned vegetable oil company. In the last two decades, it has been transformed into a professionally managed firm that derives a significant part of its revenue through software services delivered from both onshore and offshore locations. The software industry has generated a large number of well-paying jobs for young, technically qualified, Indian software professionals and this in turn has led to a booming real estate and restaurant industry. Bangalore now has a number of self-service supermarket chain stores catering to the needs of a busy workforce often comprised of two-income families who prefer ready-to-eat foods.

There is little doubt that Bangalore will continue to be at the fore-front of the Indian economy and will be increasingly crucial to the Indian government's plans for a multifold increase in India's software exports. Bangalore is also relatively well connected by air and rail to other major Indian cities, with over a dozen flights daily to Mumbai alone. Recently Lufthansa has introduced a direct connecting flight to the United States from Bangalore via Frankfurt.

Mumbai

Considered to be one of the most entrepreneurial of Indian cities, Mumbai has been dominated for centuries by forward-looking business families. The most-noted of these has been the House of Tata—a business conglomerate with billions of dollars in annual revenue. The company's operations span a wide range of industries from tea and soap to steel and heavy engineering.

Mumbai is known for its film industry and perhaps for this reason has come to be referred to as "Bollywood."

Mumbai, or Bombay, is known for its film industry and perhaps for this reason has come to be referred to as *Bollywood*. It has also had a colorful note in history. The city was offered as "dowry" when the Portuguese princess, Catherine of Braganza, was offered in marriage to the British royal family.

Mumbai is built on a series of islands just off the west coast of India. The city has an accessible and successful seaport. It also has the largest commercial airport in the country, with many daily connections to both Europe and the Far East. The commercial nature of the city has led to a cosmopolitan workforce. Furthermore, the city's transportation system of surface trains and buses, while heavily used, has the reputation for efficiency and running on time. A number of proposals have been made for improving traffic movement around the city and a "new" twin city has also been built across a creek north of Mumbai to ease congestion. With a population of close to 20 million in the metropolitan area, Mumbai is destined to remain one of world's most populated cities, as well as the financial and commercial center of the Indian economy.

Kolkata

Kolkata is one of the oldest of India's big cities, and for a while, it served as the center of the British colonial government in India. Located at the mouth of the Hooghly River, which provides Kolkata with port access to the Bay of Bengal, it was the main center of the tea and jute trade, two of India's major export items during colonial times. Today it has about 13 million people. While the city has become the symbol of India's poverty in recent decades, it is also a lively center for the arts. Its regional government was dominated for decades by a Marxist-Leninist party. Activist and disruptive trade unions led to the city and state of Kolkata developing an image of being unfriendly to private enterprise. However, in recent years, even the Communist ruling party has been seen as being interested in attracting foreign investment and the business climate has improved considerably. Kolkata is connected directly by air with India's eastern neighbors, Bangladesh and Myanmar.

The divide between the urban poor and affluent is nowhere more evident in India than in Kolkata.

The divide between the urban poor and affluent is nowhere more evident in India than in Kolkata. The missionary work of Mother Teresa which was centered around this city for over seven decades and the Hollywood film, *City of Joy,* make Kolkata a familiar name to Western audiences. While the city continues to be beset by a number of infrastructure issues and other problems of urban blight, it is also likely to be important to India's future economic development, given its strategic location and long mercantile history.

Delhi and New Delhi

The old city of Delhi together with its newer extension called New Delhi, the nation's capital, provide an interesting contrast between the old and the new in modern India. The ancient walled city of Delhi gained prominence during the rule of the various Mughal dynasties early in the second millennium, and several famous landmarks still attest to the city's glorious past. The British later established the center of national government in New Delhi and the central government of independent India still operates from the impressive cluster of

New Delhi: Paying with Plastic May Not Mean Credit Cards

Westerners rely heavily on credit cards and "paying with plastic" is the norm. However, a shortage of coins and small denomination bills in New Delhi has led various private retailer associations to produce their own currency. These brightly colored plastic coins are often used to make change below Rs 10 (US22¢). The Indian government is reported to be clearly aware of the shortage of legal coins and has even imported large numbers of newly minted coins. According to the *Financial Times,* banks often refuse to give small denomination change and bank clerks have been known to request bribes to do so. While the central bank claims there is no coin shortage, *The Hindu,* a national newspaper, refers to the plastic coins as a "parallel currency." The inventive shopkeepers in the capital city are not willing to lose sales due to something as minor as a shortage of legal tender.

Source: Angus Donald, "Retailers Short-Changed by Rupee," *Financial Times,* October 14/15, 2000, p. 4.

....

government buildings that was built toward the end of the British era.

More recently, a number of new industrial firms have been established around Delhi in the neighboring states of Haryana and Uttar Pradesh. Delhi is also the principal large city with close ties to two of the leading successful agricultural states of Haryana and Punjab. Over the 50 years of independence, these two states have made the greatest strides in raising agricultural productivity and reducing rural poverty. Delhi had a population of about 12 million in 2000.

New Delhi is the center of the diplomatic corps. With a central government bureaucracy drawing employees from across India, the city also has a cosmopolitan complexion. The climate in the region tends to be marked by extremes with night temperatures in the winter hovering around the freezing mark and day temperatures in the summer rising as high as 110 to 120 degrees Fahrenheit.

As the capital city of India, New Delhi will continue to be an important area in which foreign businesses will want to maintain a presence.

This is especially true as the liberalization continues and the central government comes to grips with crucial decisions regarding privatization of public enterprises as well as other issues posed by a more open economy and membership in the World Trade Organization.

Hyderabad

As noted earlier, Hyderabad along with Bangalore, is one of the fastest growing urban areas in the country and each city is vying with the other for the information technology investments that have been pouring into India in recent years. For now Bangalore has the clear lead in the size of its information technology industry and software exports. However, Hyderabad—often referred to as *Cyberabad* in this context—has been trying to gain a higher profile, an effort led by the Chief Minister of the Andhra Pradesh province in which it is located. Although the Chief Minister comes from a regional party whose main base is only in that province, his party is part of the ruling coalition in New Delhi. As a consequence he wields a considerable amount of influence. Several U.S. firms, including Motorola, have decided to locate major centers in Hyderabad. The city has also succeeded in attracting the Indian Business School set to open in 2001. As mentioned in Chapter 3, the school offers graduate level courses in business with the active support of high profile U.S. sponsors such as the consulting firm, McKinsey.

Located in south central India, Hyderabad has mild winters and warm summers. It is considered to have several of the attributes that have made Bangalore successful in the information technology industry, including a supportive political climate and a large supply of well-educated and technically qualified workers. Hyderabad, with a population of about 8 million, has a number of scientific and research establishments. For this reason, it and Bangalore are expected to remain at the leading edge of the information technology industry in India.

Chennai

Last, but not least, is Chennai which is located on the southeastern coast of India on the Bay of Bengal. Because of its port and long history of being a principal administrative headquarters during British rule, the city has long been regarded as an intellectual capital of South India. Chennai has been an important point of commercial activity as well. It has a number of major manufacturing industries including those producing rolling stock for the country's massive railway network, commercial trucks, and buses. The city and its province have been marked by fractious political infighting among regional parties, but its public services have always been considered better than those in many other parts of the country.

These cities will set the trends in future consumption patterns for the country.

The city is served by an international airport with good connections to points in South East Asia. Over several decades, expatriates from Chennai have established themselves successfully at various locations in such East Asian countries as Singapore and Malaysia. If India's economy continues to grow and prosper Chennai will be a natural place for commercial interchange between India and points east.

Cities as Entry Points

Most foreign firms that want to enter India will do so via one or more of the large cities we have profiled. These are also the cities that will set the trends in future consumption patterns for the country.

There is little question that consumption behavior is changing rapidly in India and many of the interviews conducted for this book, with U.S. firms operating in India, confirm this observation. With the advent of multichannel global television in India and the growing size and purchasing power of the middle class, forces are in motion that will create a great opportunity for a number of firms from within and outside India.

A survey commissioned by *India Today*,[1] a weekly newsmagazine published from New Delhi but also distributed in Canada, the United Kingdom, and the United States, provides some interesting facts. First, it is reported that in the next five years, 59.9 percent of the Indian population is expected to have an annual income of between Rs 22,501 (US$500) and Rs 70,000 (US$1,500). These incomes do not approach the affluence found in the West, even accounting for differences in purchasing power, but compared with just a decade or two ago, they do represent a significant increase in purchasing power. The *India Today* article estimates that within the next five years, the upper income population earning more than Rs 70,000 annually (over US$1,500) will comprise 22.3 percent of the population.

The *India Today* survey goes on to report the results of a five-city comparison (the same cities described earlier with the exception of Hyderabad) of relative earnings between 1990 and 2000. In this comparison, Delhi showed the greatest increase in families with monthly incomes over US$150 while Chennai also showed a healthy increase. Kolkata showed a small increase; Bangalore stayed about the same. Mumbai showed a small decline although the decline put it only second to Delhi.

There were also interesting differences among the cities in the types of housing occupied by survey respondents and in the patterns of ownership of appliances and vehicles. Specifically, the largest shares of people who owned their places of residence were in Delhi and in Bangalore, whereas Kolkata had the highest number of respondents who had inherited their homes. In Chennai and Mumbai significant percentages of respondents had accommodations provided by their employers. Both Bangalore and Chennai also had large numbers of renters.

Color TVs were the most-owned item in 2000 (85 percent). In 1990, electric irons ranked first with 86 percent. The preferred mode of saving also varied somewhat among cities. Bank deposits were the most preferred in Delhi, Chennai, and Mumbai, whereas property was most preferred in Bangalore, and insurance was the most preferred in Kolkata. A precise explanation for this pattern of preferred savings instruments is unclear. It should also be remembered that the data recorded only ordinal preferences and the differences may be less than the rankings alone indicate. We also noted that although respondents were generally optimistic about the future, there was still some insecurity expressed. This may explain why more than one-half the respondents

Color TVs were the most-owned item in 2000 (85 percent). In 1990, electric irons ranked first with 86 percent.

still saved fully one fourth of their income. This high savings rate no doubt has a silver lining in that it represents a large pool of potential investment funds that the economy could use if current liberalization efforts continue.

NOTE

1. "Better Off Than Dad, The New Economy Opinion Poll," *India Today*, February 19, 2001, pp 37–40.

CHAPTER 7

Speaking from Experience:
Caterpillar India

This case study is based upon an interview with Mr. Don DaSaro, Commercial Director for Earth Moving and Mining, Caterpillar India on April 10, 2001. Mr. DaSaro has worked in Asia intermittently for 30 years, living in Hong Kong, Indonesia, Malaysia and Singapore. He has lived in India the past six years.

Background

We are a heavy-equipment manufacturer with facilities around the world. Our products are merchandised through independently owned Caterpillar dealerships that have been established in virtually every country in the world. Our entry into the market generally is through the dealer mechanism.

This dealer approach differs from an agency (or distributor) approach in that an agency is a representative of the principal, whereas the dealer is wholly owned and independent. We have a contractual arrangement, including sales and service, which defines the manner in which dealers can represent us. The result of this practice has been the ability to build durable relationships over the years. In India, one dealer has worked with us for nearly 60 years, since 1948. A second dealership was started in 1987.

We make our manufacturing entry decisions country-by-country, based on whether a country has the economic system, infrastructure and a sufficient demand for our products. Here in India, we have one licensee arrangement and one joint venture operation. Our licensee arrangement, with Hindustan Motor, began in 1988–89. Our joint venture arrangement with Hindustan Power began at about that same time.

Everything in India is very slow. Changes of government (instability) and political unrest frequently disrupt business. For instance, between 1995 and 1999, I believe there were four different governments, which delayed any long-term plans we had within India. Good business thrives on predictability, which is not to be found in India yet. On the other hand, each government during this time seemed to have an amiable outlook to business. The problem with these frequent changes was not so much that there was vacillation in the government's willingness to participate, but more in the uncertainties and which form participation would take.

In terms of people and know-how, Indians are very well educated, with high levels of skill.

In terms of people and know-how, Indians are very well educated, with high levels of skill. In my view, it seems India is not looking so much towards Asia for development and markets, as it is looking more towards Western markets. So its ideas are more westernized in that process.

India is quite familiar with free enterprise since it is one of the oldest democracies in Asia. Although it has a free enterprise system, generally speaking, there are still quite a few state-owned operations. The government is now realizing that these are not viable. Far from being profitable, they are a drain on the government's coffers. Fortunately, private sector business, represented by the Confederation of Indian Industry (CII), has had the ear of the government and has prevailed in terms of attempting to develop the private sector.

Distribution System

India's distribution system is very poor. It has been greatly hampered by the lack of infrastructure. Inadequate roads and poor communication systems are holding India back today. There are plans to improve both. Communications will certainly improve when fiber optics is put to use.

Competitive Environment

The competitive environment is extremely intense, especially in the growing area of free enterprise in non-governmental sectors. Overall, there is a tendency toward capacity marketing. That is, if a plant has a certain production capacity, it is going to produce at that maximum level regardless of pricing because volume is the issue and not necessarily profitability.

Management Style

The style is dominated by Western influence. There are people here running companies that have been educated in the best universities around the world and they bring in tremendous skills from the combination of natural ability and training. But there is still a fair amount of government influence that comes into play—which has no management style.

Size of the Middle Class

The size of the middle class is probably less than 10 percent of the total population. In terms of volume or gross number, this is very impressive, but when you look at it in relation to the rest of India, it probably does not have as much impact as we might hope. The question really is will the middle class grow above its current level? It is my opinion that it will grow, albeit slowly.

I do think that the term "middle class" needs to be redefined. What are the definitions of its purchasing power and yearly income? Once you get to that definition, then the middle class is not very different from the middle class anywhere else, in terms of making the transition from bike, to motorcycle, to automobile, to better automobile. It's the same with homes and consumer goods. You see a lot of white goods in the media today and apparently they are doing reasonably well. How that filters down to the countryside, of course, becomes another issue. Many rural people do not have electricity or running water. They can neither afford nor use these new consumer goods.

Marketing Approach

We market our equipment through our Caterpillar dealers. Building a road in India is essentially the same as building a road anywhere, so our marketing approach is the same. The factors that change it, of course, are pricing levels, financing, and product support. This also is tied in to the distribution system because of the unique nature of the Caterpillar dealers. We place a great deal of emphasis on distribution and product support and parts availability and servicing. This philosophy, or marketing approach, holds true whether we are in India, China, or anywhere else in the world. The rate of speed and application are the only differences worldwide.

Marketing and Advertising

We do not advertise to create primary demand. That is, we do not advertise directly to consumers about the need for better roads, nor do we encourage customers to push the government for improved infrastructure. There is enough pressure from other sources. We, as a multinational, hold ourselves at arm's length from any type of activity along those lines. We would expect our independent dealer organizations to do that, if required. The need for infrastructure in India is so obvious to the population that there is no need to develop a specific marketing plan or approach for it.

Marketing Process

Caterpillar advertisements are aimed at a global market using such venues as CNN and *Time* magazine, for example. Our ads are more focused on our contribution to the overall economy of a country rather than on specific products. We leave it up to local dealers to advertise appropriately, as required, for specific models. This of course varies from country to country. One country or area may have more need of equipment for agricultural type activities, while others need to know about logging or mining or land clearing equipment. In India, we focused mainly on mining.

Standardization of Product

Our product is both standardized and localized to suit Indian conditions. We have around 350 machine and engine models available to the market here, some of which cannot be localized. They are standardized products, no matter what. For example, we may add or subtract air-conditioning. We try to de-feature machines in some locations. If we have sophisticated electronics on a model that has been used in various parts of the world successfully, then we'll try to introduce it here. But if customers are not willing to pay extra for it, then we'll localize it by removing some of the costly features to bring the price down. We localize to that extent.

We sell to the demand. In the past, India has been a predominantly a mining market for us, with Coal India and other big mines like Hindustan Copper being our main customers. Now there is an upsurge in multilateral funding—World Bank, Asian Development Bank (ADB) and others—for road construction. So, we will start producing, assembling and selling equipment for the road construction industry.

Reasons for Selling a Standardized Product

A product becomes standardized when we find that there is not much that can be added or deleted from the product to yield the type of profit levels the end user hopes to achieve with it. What is the driver behind localization? The main driver is whether the attachments and benefits of various components of the machinery can yield or fetch the price that we have set up for the product. If it cannot, then of course the customer will not pay for the product and its attachments. They do not need it badly enough to pay for it. There is no demand for it; therefore, we do not offer it.

Cultural Differences

The managers we run into in our business, as stated earlier, have been trained in one form or another in Western countries, so there is a considerable amount of similarity. Differences are most pronounced in areas with a general focus, and in organizations that don't have much business with the West. There is not a high level of tolerance for ambiguity. Everybody wants to know who is going to authorize a particular action, and there is a great deal of paperwork associated with the bureaucratic nature of it all. Individual achievement is highly valued. People like to be successful and India has many entrepreneurs. There is high differentiation between men and women, although there are not many women in our end of the business.

There is a capacity for teamwork here once goals and objectives are defined and the right people are in place. Once you have clearly defined the direction to go toward, then you can let people have their go at it with good results.

Comparison with China

India is far more attractive to us, in my estimation, for a number of reasons. China does not have the structure, either politically or financially, to sustain itself. In China, the government still controls most business. India enjoys more free enterprise, with its growing public sector getting out of Nehruvian politics. India has good civil laws, a good commercial code, a court system where people's complaints can be heard, and of course, a very strong financial system. And, of course, the fluency of English is greater in India than in most parts of China.

China does have more purchasing power, as far as that goes, because it is bigger. I don't know the exact number, but nearly 60 percent of India is still agrarian. That in itself sets the standard. The comparison should be made from the portion of India, which is not agrarian in nature; rather look at the five major cities to make a comparison. However, across the board generally, I would have to agree that China has more purchasing power.

Projections and Challenges

We think the market will continue to grow. In fact, we are very bullish on it. We just spent US$85 million to buy a manufacturing plant in Chennai. As far as challenges, infrastructure is the main issue, in a "good news, bad news" sort of way. The bad news is that we have to deal with it. The good news is that it presents us with an opportunity. So, we will focus our efforts on the development of infrastructure.

Another challenge is bureaucracy. The length of time it takes to get any infrastructure project initiated, underway, and completed is an area of great frustration, whether it's an airport, road or port upgradation. When I arrived in 1995, there were eight fast-track projects on the government's list. They were all to go ahead, no matter what. Enron was the first one, and they are still stalled after six years. The other seven have not even come up. This is bad for business in India. It is hard for countries to develop if they are missing the basic services.

CHAPTER 8

India's Middle Class: Mirage or Reality?

THE Indian middle class has acted as a beacon to many multinational investors interested in capturing a slice of this huge and growing segment that can be counted in the millions. Interestingly, there is no consensus on the size of the middle class and in general, its definition is too vague to be meaningful to a foreign investor seeking to market goods and services in India. In this section, we take a look at this attractive, yet elusive class of consumers, and try to provide some perspective on their potential as present and future consumers of products and services.

Many multinational investors entered India after the country's liberalization. At the time analysts estimated the size of the middle class at around 150 to 300 million. They now realize that their initial estimates of the size of India's middle class, as well as its purchasing power, were far from realistic. In some cases, their woes were compounded by lackluster growth and anemic sales. The initial estimates are more in line with today's population projections.

That is the darker side of the picture. On a more positive note, India is a market in transition with attractions that include a large and growing domestic market, a large pool of scientific and technical talent, a strong and growing information technology sector, and a high level of entrepreneurial energy. In fact, current reforms have a gone a long way toward creating an investor-friendly environment by streamlining the foreign investment approval process and by liberalizing regulations.[1]

Historically, under a post-independence government that emphasized development of heavy industry over consumer goods, the Indian middle class consumer was starved of choice and quality in consumer goods. In the days of the *license raj* discussed in Chapter 2, the consumer was held captive to producer interests. Producers benefited from government protectionism, while simultaneously suffering the many restrictions of a heavy-handed government and its bureaucratic regulations.

The economic reforms of the past decade, coupled with growing numbers of dual-income households, have vastly increased the purchasing power of today's middle class consumers, as well as their desire to consume. Given better quality and selection, these starved consumers are buying consumer goods to satisfy pent-up demand and to exercise their newly found power of choice. It is not an exaggeration to say that a new wave of consumerism is sweeping the country. The old mentality of saving for a rainy day is slowly, but surely, giving way to a new one of measured indulgence in some of the consumer luxuries. Purchases such as color television sets, washing machines, and even personal computers that are commonplace in the United States, Canada, and the European Union are becoming more common in India. Today, a middle class family may take out a bank loan to buy a personal computer, which is used both for educating their children and for the home.

It is not an exaggeration to say that a new wave of consumerism is sweeping the country.

In this chapter, we offer insights on India's middle class from a cross-section of executives from leading U.S. consumer goods firms with operations in India. These insights were gained through a series of in-depth interviews conducted either in person or over the telephone over a two-year period, 1999–2001. Many of the executives interviewed have had significant experience in India. This section presents their perspectives on the nature and size of the Indian middle class, along with marketing insights they have gleaned from their experience in India.

The Indian Bottled Water Market

One of the fastest growing and most hotly contested businesses in India is the water business. Included among the firms competing for the estimated Rs 700 core market are a number of companies that are household names in the U.S. and Europe. These include Coca-Cola with its Kinley brand and Pepsi Foods India with its Aquifina brand. Among the other well-known competitors are Nestlé and Evian, but a local product, Bisleri, has an estimated 60 percent market share. *India Today* estimates that there are 500 players in this growing market.

Source: Renuka Methil, "Liquid Asset," *India Today,* May 14, 2001, pp. 32–33.

....

Size and Definition

The business press variously estimates the size of India's middle class anywhere from 150 to 300 million people. With an average household size of 5, this translates into 30,000 to 60,000 households. Many multinationals originally drawn into the country by the seduction of large markets later discovered that the numbers were somewhat misleading. A U.S. Department of Commerce Report states:

> Only the 11 million households in the upper and upper middle classes make up a market for most consumer durables and luxury items, which in the Indian context may be items that are quite commonplace in developed countries. These households would include about 40 to 50 million people. The middle and lower strata of the middle class, however, can be included in the market for consumable items like cosmetics, toiletries, processed foods and entertainment, though their consumption levels will be modest.[2]

This illustrates how the tendency to use the term middle class in its broadest sense can prove to be a problem. One should not conjure up a picture of the buying activity of U.S. middle-class consumers when referring to India.

Most Western consumer goods firms focus primarily on the more affluent high potential urban consumers.

Our interview research reveals that at least for marketing to India's urban population, two key segments stand out. The first is an American-style, urban, middle class of about 8 to 10 million households. These consumers are brand conscious and are prepared to pay a high price for well-known global brands. The other outstanding segment is an Indian-style, urban, middle class of about 45 to 50 million households. These consumers buy Western-style products, but are still too price conscious to purchase with frequency consumer products offered by Western multinational companies. Beyond these middle class consumers, however, is the large, relatively poor, rural and urban population that purchases only the barest necessities and few consumer goods. What is important therefore, is for most Western consumer goods firms to focus primarily on the more affluent high potential urban consumers and to rely on market segmentation to determine the market's potential for their specific product. As noted, multinational managers have a mental definition of the middle class rooted in a Western context and sometimes tend to view the middle class in emerging markets using their familiar frame of reference. This leads to miscalculations of the size and purchasing power of the middle class in markets such as India.[3] However, although now small, their numbers are growing rapidly and as the country's economic fortune improves, urban middle class consumers in India could be a target segment for products that currently have much broader appeal in the United States. A Pillsbury executive emphasizes this point saying:

> You have to be careful what you define as the middle class. Technically, if you look at the middle class in the 1990s, when they opened the country and multinationals flooded in, they all had a magical number of 250 to 270 million people. But, if you step back for a moment, out of a total population of 1 billion people, you have only 290 million people in urban India. Anyone entering the country for the first 5 to 10 years should look only at urban India.

How does one define a middle class consumer in India, given the vast differences in income levels and purchasing power relative to Western markets? Using income alone in the Indian context is an insufficient, even misleading indicator of the ability to purchase goods and services. One study defined each group by using criteria other than household income. Instead its definitions relied on criteria such as urban and rural differences, the level of education, the type of housing, and possession of selected durable goods.[4] Some have used electricity bills as indicators of consumption and others, such as Procter & Gamble, use simple lifestyle indicators to identify good sales prospects. For example, do they have a refrigerator or water filter? Another factor related to consumer buying power is the large number of successful Indian nationals (or former nationals) who live in the United States, Canada, and Europe. Many of these Non-Resident Indians (NRIs) send financial gifts—sometimes sizeable amounts—to their relatives in India. It is difficult to estimate these amounts and their impact on the middle-income equation.

Executive Perceptions of Market Potential

All the executives saw the emerging market in India as an important one and perceived excellent long-term potential. However, their impressions of the market in the near term are tempered by the difficulties of doing business in an economy in the throes of transition from a relatively closed to a more open market.

The consensus is that while India is not an easy place to do business, the long term prognosis is great. Most firms plan to persevere until the going gets easier. For instance, William Wrigley Jr. Company entered India in the past five years, but business has not developed as expected in India, since the habit of gum-chewing is not widespread. Per capita consumption of gum in India is low relative to the United States and culture could be an important variable in how readily Indian people accept the habit of gum chewing. In this regard India is a tough market. In spite of these difficulties, Doug Barrie, President, Wrigley International states, "What makes India attractive is the sheer magnitude of its potential. India is a country you cannot afford not to be in. Our challenge is to find a way to get more people to chew gum."

Roger Hagstrom, Director of Marketing-Asia Region for Goodyear Company, sees India as "a marketplace in transition." He recognizes that there will be near-term twists and turns with this growing economy, along with the promise of long term profits. Goodyear has been in India since 1922 and its image is so local that one of its marketing problems is having too local a face in a country where imported goods have positive country-of-origin effects. Mr. Hagstrom sees a growing similarity between middle-class Indians and U.S. and European consumers and attributes this to the influence of global communication networks like the Internet and cable television. These media have a homogenizing influence on the world in terms of tastes and preferences.

He adds, "The middle class in India is growing and with a growing economy free of government intervention, their numbers will increase. This rising middle class will want cars and better roads and may put pressure on the government to supply better infrastructure in terms of roads, power, and telecommunications, all of which are in short supply. The middle class segment in India is globalizing, but the rural segment is different."

India has two different markets: a localized one with modest incomes and a Westernized one with higher income levels.

Ken Justice, Director of International Marketing Intelligence for Diebold Inc., which sells ATMs in India, concurs with the increasing power of the middle class. He says, "India has a huge middle class in terms of raw numbers and the ATM opportunity lies with this group which the private banks are targeting. The middle class with its growing purchasing power will look for more convenience-oriented delivery channels." Interestingly, he adds that, in general "the Indian consumer is similar, but similar to U.S. consumers back in the early 1970s on the trust issue. There is the customer segment that is served by the private banks, a lot of them are well traveled, maybe educated abroad, and they could have a different level of trust in the ATMs. But the masses in India are at a very different level of trust."

Miles Greer of Sara Lee also talked about the bifurcated Indian market. In his words, "India has two different markets: a localized one with modest incomes and a Westernized one with higher income

India's burgeoning cable TV industry is outstripping China

Nearly one-half of the 70 million Indian homes that currently have TV have cable. Moreover, India has an estimated 30,000 to 50,000 cable operators. It is the third largest cable market in the world; exceeded only by the U.S. and China. Given these staggering statistics, it is not surprising that it has become a battleground for an increasing number of channels questing for viewers. While China has a limited number of channels—CNN is available in Western-style hotels—an Indian family can receive 85 channels for a monthly $3.26 cable TV fee. Already a leader in the movie industry with Bollywood setting a frantic pace for firm production, India is fast becoming a TV leader. Among the global channels in India are MTV India, CNBC India, CNN, FTV (France), and Murdoch's Star TV. Programs like *Suddenly Susan, Ally McBeal,* and *Baywatch,* have joined cricket matches, mythological serials, and game shows as regular viewing fare. There were at least ten mythological serials alone on the air in Spring 2001. The number of cable TV homes is forecast to reach 40 million by the middle of this decade.

Sources: Lander, Mark, "A Glut of Cable TV in India," *The New York Times,* March 23, 2002, p. C1 and C 12; Renuka Methil, "Banking on Faith," *India Today,* April 16, 2001, p. 44; Anna M. M. Vetticad, "Life after Crorepati," *India Today,* May 28, 2001, p. 42

....

levels. Sara Lee's approach would vary for the two groups. Different market segments exist in the United States as well, but in India it is more pronounced."

These comments from executives at leading U.S. multinationals corroborate the existence of cross-national consumer segments in the United States and India. The Indian segment that is willing and able to buy Western brands, albeit small at present, exists and is growing. As an executive at Dana, a leading global supplier of automotive parts, puts it, "We characterize, and continue to characterize India as a very strong growth market. Dana has sort of equated India and Brazil as very strong growth markets in terms of potential size and critical mass. The current thinking is that India may take a while longer to get there than previously thought. Yet the long-term perspective is good."

Marketing to India's Middle Class

The middle class in India is far from homogenous. It is different in many ways compared with its Western counterpart in terms of purchasing power, consumer tastes, preferences, and value systems. Yet, several executives perceived similarities between the upper segment of the middle class in India and the middle class in the U.S. in terms of brand recognition and to some extent purchasing power. Hence, many of the multinational entrants tended to target the upper end of the market in order to capture the benefits of their standardized global brands.

Many of the multinational entrants tended to target the upper end of the market in order to capture the benefits of their standardized global brands.

A Ford Motor Company executive told us that India's middle class compares with the U.S. since ". . . they are looking for items in their lives to fulfill a need—the transportation need, or a psychological need for a bigger and better car." In his view, compared with Americans, consumers in India are more price-sensitive and do more research before purchasing big-ticket items. This is understandable since they have a shorter history of making major purchases. Middle-class consumers in India are willing to spend on consumer items, but do not spend indiscriminately. Hence, they take a longer time to make decisions and spending levels are nowhere near U.S. levels.

In a similar vein, a Procter & Gamble executive sees similarities at the upper end between consumers in the U.S. and India. In his words:

> At the upper end at least, you can take a standardized approach, because the upper end is globally literate, they watch global TV channels such as Star TV, they drive global brand-name cars, they use global brand name washing machines. Indians at the top end also want big refrigerators, just like the Americans.

In our interviews with them, the executives emphasized the need to accommodate cultural differences in marketing to the middle class. For instance, India is a country where extended family structures are still prevalent and group size is bigger. In order to accommodate this aspect of the culture, a McDonald's executive pointed out that his firm's commercials for India are modified to include extended family

McDonald's and an Indian crisis

On May 4, 2001, McDonald's found itself with a crisis in Mumbai and New Delhi. It had been reported in the U.S. the previous day that the company had been using oil with a beef extract to cook its fries. Word quickly spread to India where Hindu and vegetarian customers were shocked and concerned, since eating beef-related products is forbidden to them.

Angry mobs assaulted several McDonald's outlets in the two major Indian cities. Fortunately, the firm's crisis management team was able to quickly initiate a media campaign and local (Indian) laboratory tests to assure the public that there was no animal fat used in Indian fries. Thus, McDonald's averted further vandalism and protests and demonstrated its cultural sensitivity to its Hindu and vegetarian customers. As one of the world's highest profile companies, negative press for McDonald's anywhere in the world becomes a local issue and calls for a local response.

Source: Sarika Gupte, "McDonald's Averts a Crisis," *adageglobal,* July 2001, p. 4.

....

members. This is true both when showing pictures of the restaurant, as well as when telling the story in the commercials. In addition to selling a standardized product menu in India, McDonald's has developed a few unique products to suit local taste, such as the Maharaja Mac, a non-beef burger and the Pizza Puff, a pastry with Indian filling. The executive explains:

> We have developed this product [Pizza Puff] uniquely for India. In that sense India has been unique for us. In no other country have we depended on new products to this extent. In other countries, we normally open up with a standardized menu and maybe after a while as a promotional thing we introduce new products. In India, the core consists of new products.

Most firms entering India view the middle class in terms of a pyramid, consisting of three to five tiers, depending on the type of product. Some use income to segment this class, others use lifestyle characteristics for consumer durables such as automobiles. Usage studies help to identify segments for consumer non-durables like Gillette razors and Kellogg's cereals. Almost all the firms targeted the upper end of the middle class spectrum with relatively standardized products, modified to some extent to suit local culture and environment. The firms' target market size in nearly all cases was a function of the type of product. For instance, Ford Motor Company's target market is the upper peak of the pyramid amounting to roughly 10 to 15 million customers. Procter & Gamble, which sells consumer packaged goods estimates a much larger figure as its target.

Firms also consider the "affordability issue" in developing and pricing products for the Indian market. McDonald's takes the price-sensitivity of the Indian consumer into account when setting prices for its products. Its target market is the A, B, and C class of consumers on an A to E scale, where A is the most affluent. Xerox, selling copiers in India, eliminated some "bells and whistles" to make the products more affordable to consumers.

A U.S. government study reports:

> "Foreign companies have tried to overcome this price consciousness by promoting the concept of value to Indian consumers: You pay more, but you receive a higher quality product. To date, the results have been mixed. Price, not value, seems foremost on the minds of most consumers here."[5]

Many of the firms interviewed seemed to strike a balance between standardizing and localizing their products and promotions. The upper end of the middle class is rooted in Indian culture, yet globally literate, and exposed to Western brands via travel and media. Their level of familiarity with global brands makes it feasible for Western firms to pursue a premium pricing strategy with relatively standardized global products, but in most cases the price-value equation needs to be reviewed for the Indian market.

Notes

1. Ganguli, Amal and Michalla Siren, "Approaching India: A Guide for Investors," *Price Waterhouse Review,* June 1996, 26–45.

2. "India: Indian Market," *International Trade Data Network IMI Reports,* http://www.ITDN.net/cgi-bin.

3. Prahalad, C. K. and Kenneth Lieberthal, "The End of Corporate Imperialism," *Harvard Business Review,* July-August 1998.

4. "India: Indian Market," *International Trade Data Network IMI Reports,* http://www.ITDN.net/cgi-bin.

5. "Marketing: Some Thoughts and Pitfalls" *Country: India, Asia Pacific Database,* p 3–4. http://infoserv2.ita.doc.gov.

CHAPTER 9

Strategies for Doing Business in India

NEARLY every issue of *The Wall Street Journal, Business Week, Fortune* or other mainstream U.S. or Canadian business publication carries an announcement of another large investment in China. Moreover, this direct investment momentum was further accelerated by Congress' granting of "normal trade relations" with China in mid-2000.

In less dramatic fashion and certainly with less publicity, many U.S. and Canadian businesses have either established themselves in India or at least begun to take an interest in the country. For example, in November 1999, Ford introduced an Indian-produced mid-size car—the Ikon—specifically designed for the Indian subcontinent. Likewise, many U.S. software firms have established Indian subsidiaries. The *Financial Times* has been a particularly valuable source in recording this "move to India" by major U.S. business firms. This is perhaps due to the Britain's long-term involvement in the country, which is reflected in the newspaper's coverage.

In order to get a clearer picture of U.S. firms' interests in India, the nature of their entry strategy, and their marketing approaches, we did our own research. Over the past five years, we have conducted two studies designed to answer key questions regarding the way U.S. firms have chosen to do business in this exciting market. Let's look at the results in some detail.

Entry Form

Our first study was directed largely at determining the form of entry that U.S. firms were employing in India, (i.e. joint venture, acquisition,

Rise in Asian Imports

India's potential for consumer product sales has been strongly recognized by Asian marketers, according to a report in *India Today*. What is troubling for Indian producers, however, is that the Asian goods are beating local firms in terms of both price and quality. Wrist watches, toys, sport shoes, pocket radios, dry cell batteries, and CD players are among the thousands of articles arriving daily from China, Singapore, and Taiwan. In fact, many Indian companies themselves are now outsourcing in the Far East in order to take advantage of the lower costs and product quality

Many Indian companies and trade associations, such as the Association of Indian Dry Cell Manufacturers, have initiated anti-dumping investigations or have sought other forms of government protection. Imports of electronic products from China alone grew from $52 million in 1996–97 to $176 million in 1999–2000 and the totals continue to rise.

Further, India's current customs and countervailing duties are not adequate to make the Asian products more expensive than the locally produced products. For example, Chinese wrist watches are priced in the store at less than one-third the nearest Indian-produced equivalent. Observers feel that the Indian government's hands are tied due to WTO rules and the country's desire to keep friendly relations with China and the other East Asian countries. Consumers seem to be the winners in all this, especially those in the major markets.

The lesson for U.S. and European producers is that there is a ready acceptance of new and innovative products in India, especially distinctive ones that are competitively priced.

Source: V. Shankar and Rohit Saran, "Taste of China," *India Today*, December 11, 2000, p. 27–31.

....

or a greenfield operation—creating an entirely new plant that is wholly owned by the MNC). Based primarily on business newspaper and magazine reports, we determined the entry strategies employed by 30 U.S. MNCs, including Ford, Hewlett-Packard and Coca-Cola. As shown in Figure 9.1, virtually all the firms chose to enter the Indian market through either a joint venture or a greenfield operation.

FIGURE 9.1 INDIA ENTRY APPROACH

ACQ = Acquisition; GF = Greenfield; JV = Joint Venture

Company	Mode of Entry	Industry/Product
Coca-Cola	ACQ	Soft drinks
DuPont	GF	X-ray film
Kellogg's	GF	Cereals/Food Processing
GM	GF	Mid-size Vehicles
Hewlett-Packard	GF	Electronics
General Electric	JV	White goods/Plastics
Ford	JV	Auto-radiators
IBM	JV	Hardware/Software
Procter & Gamble	JV	Soaps/Detergents
Bausch & Lomb	GF	Contact lenses/Sunglasses
Texas Instruments	GF	Computers
McDonald's	GF	Fast Food
Burger King	GF	Fast Food
KFC	GF	Fast Food
Pizza Hut	GF	Pizza
Pepsi	JV	Soft drinks
Cargill	GF	Fertilizers/Seeds
Johnson & Johnson	GF	Consumer goods
Gillette	JV	Shaving products
Timex	JV	Quartz watches
AT&T	JV	Telephone Switchboards
Tetley's	JV	Instant Teas
Honeywell	JV	Computers
Digital	GF	Computers
3M	JV	Computer networking equipment
Whirlpool	JV	White goods
Duracell	JV	Batteries
Goodyear	JV	Tires
Mobil	JV	Petroleum
Alcoa	JV	Aluminum

We reported the findings of this first study in 1996 in *International Executive.* At that time, all 30 multi-national corporations were recent entrants or re-entrants to India. More than 40 percent of the firms, especially those in consumer goods and services, had chosen to use a greenfield strategy. The popularity of the greenfield was due, at least, in part, to liberalization of investment rules. By choosing a greenfield strategy, the firms showed commitment to the market, a desire to maximize economies in their production facilities, and a vote of confidence in India's economy. In some industries, firms also may have found a lack of potential partners.[1]

Fifty-three percent of the firms chose a joint venture. This strategy has been used for a long time by business-to-business firms. The popularity of joint ventures in India among this group of MNCs indicates an increased availability of partners, a desire to spread risk, and recognition of the importance of a partner with local knowledge and contacts.

Most likely to have chosen joint ventures are companies that either need large capital investments or those that are able to find a partner with significant local presence. The greenfield approach is more likely chosen by firms who want to protect their technology, or those that cannot find a significant local partner. IBM is an example of the former; fast food companies, an example of the latter.[2]

In this same article, we noted that Ford's joint-venture operation (with Maruti-Udyog) was limited at the time to producing radiators and other car components; it was primarily a business-to-business operation. Subsequently, Ford has used India as a platform for tailoring cars for the subcontinent. Its Ikon offers many Indian-specific design features.[3] By comparison, we found that General Electric, the largest U.S. investor in India at the time of our research, had invested about US$100 million in joint ventures ranging from refrigerators and washing machines (with Godrej) to plastics (with Indian Petrochemicals) and lamps (with WIPRO).

In addition, our research found that many consumer products firms, such as Procter & Gamble, Johnson & Johnson, and Gillette were in the market and were already successfully targeting the large and growing middle class. Unlike GE, which relied exclusively on joint ventures, P&G was using joint ventures, acquisitions, and greenfield modes of entry.

In 1980, P&G acquired Richardson Vicks, the manufacturer of the well-known Vicks brand of cough and cold remedies. In its first joint venture, it established Procter & Gamble Godrej, with 51 percent ownership to P&G. This venture gave it overnight entry into the soap market. Godrej brought a powerful sales and distribution network to the joint venture as well as the technology for making soaps from vegetable oils—a necessary technology because tallow is banned in India. Procter & Gamble Home Products, a 100-percent greenfield operation, was established in 1993.[4]

Another important reason we found for firms selecting India in our first study was the limited competition in the market. For example, DuPont's decision to locate its polyester film plant in India was driven by the size of the market as well as a low level of competition. A spokesperson for the subsidiary indicated that Japan had too much competition and markets like Taiwan and Singapore were too small. In contrast, India offered a huge domestic market and little competition.[5]

Overall, our initial research provided a useful picture of the strategies firms were following when entering India prior to the mid-1990s, as well as the types of firms that were entering the Indian market.

A Fresh Look at U.S. Corporate Strategy

In preparing this book, it became apparent that we needed not only to update the earlier research, but to look at more firms as well. Moreover, we wanted to know just how firms were viewing the Indian market in terms of their marketing strategy. For example, many companies prefer to use global advertising campaigns and to follow the same basic marketing strategy in every market they enter. While English is widely spoken among middle-and-upper-class Indian consumers and many travel to the U.S. and Britain and are familiar with Western products, we wanted to find out whether a global-marketing approach would work for those firms in India. We conducted both an extensive mail survey with a large sample of U.S. firms and personal interviews with the international heads of a carefully selected group of companies.

In the remainder of this chapter, we will consider the entry strategy findings from this research. Then, in the following chapter we will analyze the marketing-specific topics, (i.e. those dealing with the marketing strategy issues).

Second Study

Our second study obtained information directly from the leading corporations. The study was conducted in early 2000 and therefore, reflects India's more recent foreign-industry friendly political and economic climate.

The executives participating in our study were mostly highly experienced veterans of the international marketplace. In fact, 56 percent of them had over ten years of international experience. Moreover, most of the firms they represented do 40 percent or more of their business overseas. The bulk of the companies in our study (58 percent) were primarily business-to-business companies. The remainder were producers of consumer products.

Indian Presence

As might be expected, the majority of the firms in our study (78 percent) are currently doing business in India. Naturally, this is a higher percentage than you would find from a population of all U.S. companies. We chose firms that were active globally and typically had investment in Asia and other areas outside Europe. We knew that firms already involved in India could provide us greater insight for this book and therefore, we weighted our sample in their favor.

Of those firms involved in India, we found that nearly 40 percent (Figure 9.2) have direct investment there. The Indian government has been receptive to direct investment—either majority or 100 percent—only in the past 5 to 10 years, so these clearly represented relatively new investors. Owens-Illinois, for example, entered India less than a decade ago with a licensing agreement. It subsequently acquired its licensee and formed a joint venture with another Indian firm. Today, Owens-Illinois has turned this joint venture into a wholly owned firm. This all occurred in fewer than 10 years.

Following direct-investment entry strategy, second in popularity among the firms in our research was the joint venture entry method. Roughly one-third of the firms are using some form of joint-venture arrangement. For example, Diebold, the Canton, Ohio ATM producer, found it advantageous to enter a joint-venture arrangement because this allowed the company to employ a "screw-driver" production facility there. In other words, the ATM manufacturer brings components into the country and with its joint-venture partner, it assembles the product there. This practice permits the firm to avoid high finished goods tariffs, helps meet local content concerns, and could prove helpful in winning government contracts.

Goodyear International provides another reason to choose the joint venture method of entry. Variation in rules and regulations among the states in India adds to the already problematic distribution issues in the tire industry. Goodyear believes that its joint venture with South Asia Tyres helps it avoid many of the difficulties of the inefficient tire distribution system found in India.

FIGURE 9. 2 CURRENT MODE OF ENTRY IN INDIA

Current Mode of Entry by Percent

Export	18%
Joint Venture	32%
Direct Investment	39%
Licensing Agreement	11%

Source: Interviews conducted by authors.

Indian Pharmaceuticals and the WTO

For decades, Indian pharmaceutical firms have avoided international patent regulations. With little (if any) regard for intellectual property laws, these firms have copied the latest drugs from U.S. and European pharmaceutical houses. Moreover, they have supplied these pirated and generic medicines to third world countries at a fraction of what the major pharmaceutical firms charge. To date, the vast majority of Indian pharmaceutical houses—an estimated 23,000 firms—have combined low-cost production methods with a few local patent laws and the result has been cheap drugs. Now, however, the WTO has set a 2005 deadline for recognizing world patents. The Indian government has agreed to follow the rules. If the Indian government does follow up on its agreement, then the days of low prices—and in some instances, low quality drugs—will end.

However, since India does have low research costs and a number of high-quality scientists, it would not be surprising if a few firms will be able to successfully compete in the global drug market. A *Financial Times* article gives several examples of Indian firms that are testing new, exciting, and original medicines.

In what is perhaps the biggest test of WTO compliance, the Indian government and Western pharmaceutical companies resolve to enforce patents. Cipla Ltd. of Mumbai offered to sell AIDS drugs to Doctors Without Borders (Paris) for about 3 percent of the price charged by its patent holders. The firm says it can manufacture the products so cheaply in India because of low raw material and production costs. And, of course, it does not have the development research and extensive testing costs of the Western drug firms.

Sources: Sitarman Shanker and David Pilling, "India Seeks a Cure for the Tough Patent Laws," *Financial Times,* May 24, 2000, p. 12.; Chris Tomlinson, "India Firm Offers Cheap AIDS Drugs," *Financial Times,* February 8, 2001, p. C–3.

....

Dana and TRW had a somewhat similar reason for employing a joint-venture approach. These two large component suppliers for the auto industry initially were drawn to India by their global original equipment customers such as General Motors, Honda, and Toyota. By forming joint ventures with strong local partners, the two U.S. companies also gain access to the sizable Indian replacement-parts market.

About one-tenth of the U.S. firms have entered India through a licensing agreement with a local Indian firm. This is a bit more risky considering India's history of poor protection of intellectual property and occasional unwillingness to permit or enforce license-fee remittance. As mentioned earlier, some U.S. firms, such as Owens-Illinois, initially entered India via a licensing agreement and then moved to more direct involvement. The firm initially entered India in order to follow several of its major customers, such as Nestlé and Heinz in food and Seagrams and Brown & Forman in beverages.

Another U.S. manufacturer that employed a licensing entry strategy in India is American Greetings. While the firm has licenses in some other markets, its Indian licensing agreement is different. Archie's, its Indian licensee, obtains its design and artwork from American Greetings, but purchases its paper locally due to tariff restrictions. The licensee's royalty payment is based on its local sales. Since American Greetings uses licensing agreements in several countries, it appears unlikely to move into either a joint-venture or wholly owned position in the future.

While just 18 percent of the firms in our study currently employ an export-only approach to India, the percentage would undoubtedly be higher if we had included smaller firms in our study. Many companies prefer to test a market via export to a good local importer or distributor before committing their resources to either a joint-venture or a wholly owned subsidiary operation.

Perhaps a critical reason why so many U.S. firms have entered India through joint ventures or direct investment has been the high tariff barriers that have discouraged exporting. In fact, several firms cited the desire to avoid high tariffs and other government restriction as a reason for their local investments. Wrigley, the U.S. gum icon, provides one example of this approach. Wrigley entered India via a small plant in Bangalore in the mid-1990s after finding that the government required local production. As a Wrigley spokesman told us, its original intent was to test the market prior to local investment, as it does in other markets. Now, however, he said, lower tariffs and new investment

Tata Group: India's Leading Family Conglomerate

Giant family conglomerates have dominated the Indian private sector for over a century. As India has opened for foreign investment and begun to privatize many government businesses, the influence of such family conglomerates has begun to wane. An exception is the Tata Group, one of India's oldest and originally its largest family private enterprise.

Founded by Jamsetji Tata in 1868, the family group's operations span much of India's economy and have total sales of roughly US$8 billion. The enterprise has almost 300 companies in about 40 business sectors, including steel, truck manufacturing, hotels, software, tea, and chemicals.

Under the direction of its current chairman, Ratan Tata, the group recently launched the Indica, positioning it as the first mass market car designed and built by an Indian company. The Tata Group survived the nation's anti-monopoly legislation of the 1970s and is prepared to compete with foreign MNCs that will likely play a large role in India's future. It has been known for its paternalistic handling of its employees, often including free housing and other benefits in their pay. Over the years, the Group has formed a number of strategic alliances with large global companies, including Daimler-Benz, Cummins, IBM, and Singapore Airlines. Its 54-hotel chain, the Taj Group includes the Lexington in New York and the St. James Court in London.

According to Milton Moskowitz, author of *The Global Marketplace*, Tata family members today have less than 2 percent of the Group with public trusts controlling 80 percent of the shares. This makes the group more of a professionally managed publicly owned firm than a family group. The Tata Group, which initially played the key role in industrializing India back in the 19th century, appears to be positioning itself to compete effectively in the new India in the 21st century.

Sources: Milton Moskowitz, *The Global Marketplace*, p. 575 and p. 579; Krishna Guha, "India's Industrial Architect," *Financial Times*, June 21, 1999, p. 10; *Hoover's Handbook of World Business* 1995–96, p. 500.

....

regulations may encourage more firms to "try the Indian markets via exporting prior to establishing a production presence there." Moreover, India's emergence as a strong WTO participant will lead to further tariff reductions in the future, making exporting a more attractive option.

Entry Summary

Our most recent research on the entry strategies U.S. producers are following in India provides some valuable insight for other firms considering this market. It also offers a better understanding of the questions that should be answered before a firm decides whether to enter the Indian market.

A dozen pre-entry questions:

1. Are my competitors entering (or have they already entered) the Indian market?

2. Are market factors such as size of the middle class, disposable income, and others comparable to my domestic or other international target markets?

3. For business-to-business firms, are my key customers already there or are they planning to enter the market?

4. Is this the time to begin to build brand recognition and primary demand for my products? This was a critical consideration for Wrigley.

5. Are there likely Indian candidates for a joint venture arrangement or acquisition?

6. What is the competitive mix in the market for my products? Are the local producers, if any, popular with consumers or industrial customers?

7. How effective and accessible is the current distribution system for my products? Many U.S. food producers have been frustrated by the lack of supermarket chains in India.

8. Do the current Indian tariff levels prohibit my export products from being competitive and how soon will the situation change?

9. Will India's intellectual property laws provide adequate protection for my products and technology? Microsoft India was reported in *The Economic Times* (India) to be fighting piracy on its own software,

while working hard to swing preference for its genuine products.[6]

10. Are my products appropriate for the urban Indian culture? Rural India is not a potential market for many firms.

11. Are Indian consumers, or in the case of business-to-business or organizational customers already quite familiar with my products and brand names? Visits to the United States or gifts from Indians who live in the U.S. have made many products popular in the country.

12. What would be the tariffs or other barriers involved in bringing my production equipment into India to start my business?

The list of U.S. firms who have entered India through licensing agreements, exporting, joint ventures and wholly owned facilities grows daily. Each firm has its own unique questions to consider or factors to weigh in an entry decision. At the end of this book, we provide a list of information sources for those needing company-specific answers to the above questions for their firm.

NOTES

1. Chandrasekaran, Aruna and John K. Ryans, "U.S. Foreign Direct Investment in India: Emerging Trends in MNC Entry Strategies," *The International Executive* 38 (5) 1996, 599-612.

2. *Op. cit.*

3. Kazmin, Amy Louise and Mikii Tait, "U.S. car makers take lessons from the Indian consumer," *Financial Times,* November 22, 1999, p. 5.

4. Chandrasekaran and Ryans, p. 609.

5. Piramal, G., "Foreign Investment: More But Still Not Enough," *Financial Times,* June 26, 1992, p.14.

6. "Microsoft Hones (sic) In," *The Economic Times,* January 6-12, 1999.

CHAPTER 10

Standardization versus Localization in Marketing Efforts

Some companies find that it is to their advantage to appear to be as local as possible.

IN developing their marketing and advertising plans for global markets, many companies prefer to use similar programs in as many countries as possible. Such an approach is called standardized or global marketing. It may provide benefits such as lower marketing costs and proven plans.[1] A global marketer may use the same or similar advertising themes and media and the same advertising agency to sell the same products with the same packaging virtually worldwide. Very often, they use the same product brands in most of their markets.[2]

The opposite extreme from standardization is called localization. Some companies find that it is to their advantage to appear to be as local as possible. In contrast with those using standardized marketing efforts, marketers using a localized strategy develop advertising campaigns and themes, make significant product modifications, and use different distribution channels in virtually every market in which they operate.

Obviously, companies want to follow whichever approach is most effective in each market they enter, including India. However, the approach they choose depends on the extent of customer differences they see between India and the other global markets in which they operate. Many firms use one approach when they initially enter a country and later find it advantageous to switch approaches.

In our surveys and personal interviews we asked executives to discuss with us their marketing and promotion strategies in India. In this chapter, we share some of the information they have provided which may help you choose your own strategy for the Indian market.

Degree of Standardization

In our most recent survey of more than 60 corporations, we found that most companies tended to use similar products and media in both the U.S. and India. In particular, most firms used the same brand names in India and the U.S. Many Indian consumers have relatives in America, so they have traveled to the U.S., or they follow the American media so they are exposed to foreign brands. In fact, most firms pre-test and post-test their advertising in India, much as they do in the U.S. This is made possible by the fact that many major U.S. marketing research firms and advertising agencies have branches or affiliate relationships in India. Even the product labeling was the same for most firms.

Most firms pre-test and post-test their advertising in India, much as they do in the U.S.

Whereas some firms did not use the exact same marketing program in India, they did use the same decision-making process, conducting market research and using the same criteria for selecting media. A greater number did make slight variations in their marketing programs, sometimes in the content of their advertising or in their terms of sale.

Some Additional Insights

The degree of product, promotion (program), and process standardization employed by the firms covered the entire spectrum of approaches. In general, marketing process appeared to be far more standardized than marketing program.

Wrigley's is a good example of a company that uses a middle ground, contingency approach with some elements of standardization. Wrigley's sells a standardized product worldwide, but believes in adapting promotion to local markets. The marketing process is fairly standardized in Wrigley's case, but the marketing program is varied in response to the needs of the local market.

As for product, the chewing gum sold in India is identical to gum sold in the rest of the world. Wrigley's uses the same brand names, package design, and type of display material in every market. Such a strategy is guided by the basic philosophy of applying what has been successful in other countries.

In terms of advertising content, there is some variation. Wrigley's ads are not centrally developed and then transferred to other countries, including India. However, a similar copy strategy and message is used with flexibility for local execution, since ways of communicating the message vary from country to country. According to a Wrigley's executive, "There is some centralized guidance or direction, but with local adaptation or sensibility. The weakness in the highly centralized approach is the belief that any one agency or any one location has a monopoly on good ideas."

Fast food icon McDonald's, known for its standardized approach, uses some notable modifications in India. Its Indian restaurants offer several items from its standardized product line. However, as mentioned earlier, they offer some products specifically tailored for the Indian market. The Maharaja Mac—a burger made of mutton, not beef—was created as a concession to religious sensitivity to beef. The Pizza Puff, a flaky non-sweet pastry filled with vegetables flavored with Indian spices, is another example of a product created specifically for the Indian market. Since affordability is the key in India—even with the upper end of the market—the price point is calibrated to the local market. Promotion also is localized. As the McDonald's executive puts it,

> As for advertising and promotion, it seems we have not done anything international, apart from the sign of the store itself. Basically every single piece of communication that we have developed, has been developed locally, by a local Indian agency together with Indian partners.

He goes on to add that the commercials developed for India include extended families, reflecting the composition of the Indian family and the cultural emphasis on family-oriented activities. McDonald's thus is able to leverage the global brand equity of the golden arches to signal value and high quality, while catering to local taste and custom in both its product and promotion approaches in India.

Kellogg's strategy in India also uses a studied combination of standardization and localization with regard to its product, promotion, and process. While Kellogg's manufactures and sells its basic corn flakes in India, it also includes products uniquely adapted to local culture and taste in its lineup. In addition to its standardized cereal product, it sells a chocolate and a plain breakfast biscuit formulated specifically to suit the Indian palate. As for promotion, the firm adapts its execution to the local market, while maintaining similar marketing processes.

Government Regulation Has Its Effect

Adaptations are mandated not just by local culture and taste but also by government restrictions on imports into the country as the 3M example illustrates. The company sells Scotch Brite—one of its key products—in India. Because cellulose sponge is produced by local suppliers, the government will not allow 3M to import it. 3M, therefore, manufactures Scotch Brite locally but the product, which typically consists of a pad and a sponge attached to it, is sold in India with just the green pad. While the product is modified due to government restrictions on imports, consumer preference and price sensitivity mandate promotion modification. In the United States, the positioning for the product is that it lasts longer, is easy to use, and kills germs. In India it is promoted with the message that it uses less powder and hence saves money. In addition, the size of the product is reduced to lower the price point.

In spite of modifications to product and promotion, the firm uses similar marketing processes to take advantage of what it has learned in other parts of the world.

Goodyear: Common Advertising Themes

Goodyear uses a standardized approach throughout Asia as a way of capitalizing on pan-Asian similarities. It believes it is possible to promote and advertise its products on cable TV throughout Asia and this means common advertising themes are considered for an entire geographic region. It also means having common products with similar lifecycles in all these countries.

The challenge for Goodyear in markets like India and China is that sophisticated data collection and analysis of data are not easy or refined. Still, overall principles of marketing are the same. On the positive side, many marketing techniques that work in other parts of the world work in India as well. This applies to product planning, distribution, and bringing new products into the lifecycle.

India does present some unique challenges to the firm. To illustrate, ASEAN (Association of South East Asian Nations) is a common market where the movement of goods and products is getting easier. However, tariffs and restrictive government policies make trade with India more difficult. The distribution system is inefficient in India and the variation in rules and regulations among the Indian states further complicates distribution.

Goodyear's major impetus to standardize comes from its global customers in India, such as General Motors, Honda, and Toyota.

Goodyear's major impetus to standardize comes from its global customers in India, such as General Motors, Honda, and Toyota. India has advanced enough to be ready for global technology, and global customers like Honda and Toyota demand a globally competitive product from Goodyear. India's market consists of truck and passenger car tires. India has a lot of old cars, but auto makers are bringing in newer technology and they demand advanced radial tires. The passenger car side is growing and radializing, but the truck market may stay with the older bias-ply tires until the road structure is improved.

On Goodyear's approach to marketing process, an executive states:

> Our overall ad agency in the region is a global company. They generally look for common themes, so that we do not have 25 different ad campaigns and approaches for these different countries. However, we try to determine the degree of marketing program standardization based on local needs, attitudes, and interests. In terms of brand building, we try to do something which can reach

across the Asia region and touch a lot of cultures. We try to have one ad agency that helps us take the research and blend this into the advertising campaigns and programs which have a broad reach from a brand point of view. A combination of local and global is an important feature of being able to globalize.

Goodyear's product in the Asian region appears to have a high degree of standardization. As for the marketing process, some aspects such as the use of a global ad agency point to a rather standardized promotional approach, whereas the vagaries of the Indian distribution system calls for a fair amount of local adaptation.

Ford: A Car for India

Ford initially entered India with a fairly standardized product, but soon realized that local culture had to be taken into consideration in designing a car for the Indian market. As a Ford executive puts it:

The Ikon was promoted in India as "the josh machine" based on psychographic segmentation research of the Indian consumer.

Our product, the "Ikon" was designed and built specifically for India, with specific product characteristics for India, different suspensions, dimensions of the vehicle, larger back seat, large door openings for the rear seat. In India, people use the rear seat close to 90 percent of the time, compared to 10 percent in Europe or the United States. So we specifically designed and built it to Indian consumers and their needs.

The car was redesigned to suit Indian conditions. It was promoted in India as "the josh machine" based on psychographic segmentation research of the Indian consumer, which revealed that the primary target audience were auto enthusiasts who worked hard, played hard and lived a fun, aggressive lifestyle. Hence the "josh" campaign, which literally means "spontaneous exuberance" or "passion for life" in one of the Indian languages. The car is priced competitively and positioned relative to competitive offerings in this market. In spite of the differences in the actual promotion, marketing processes are similar and as the Ford executive states,

> Our approach to the fundamentals of developing an ad campaign, promotional approach, brand name, or product image . . . is the same between the United States and India.

Diebold: The Public Relations Route

Diebold's ATM product is fairly standardized on a global basis, but in India it has to be slightly modified to suit local market requirements. Diebold's joint venture partner in India uses local manufacturing to avoid tariffs. The Indian market requires some unique features, but does not want advanced functions. It wants basic, cash-dispensing, low-cost, no frills, reliable, good-quality machines. Since the density of ATMs is low in India, customers are still wary of trusting the machine. For instance, customers do not want to deposit cash in an envelope and wait for a statement days later. Rather, they want the machine to give instant credit, or to let them get their money back. The infrastructure

Mobile telephone service: reaching rural India

After a rather slow start, the mobile telephone industry has begun to grow rapidly. In fact, projections suggest that there will be 30 million subscribers in India by 2005.

Much of this growth is expected to occur in rural India, which currently has limited fixed line service. It is estimated that roughly 50 percent of the more than 600,000 rural villages have fixed line service. There are an increasing number of firms obtaining new licenses via government license auctions. Such telephone service increases can have a major impact on the economic development of the remote regions of the country.

Source: Saritha Rai, "In Rural India, A Passage to Wireless," *New York Times,* August 4, 2001, p. B-3.

....

issue of unreliable phone lines is making Diebold consider alternative technologies for this market. All of the above market idiosyncrasies call for product modification. Hence, Diebold's product approach in India could be described as middle ground.

Since Diebold's Indian customers are the large state-owned and private banks, rather than the end user, the company does its marketing on a one-to-one basis. Diebold divides the market into state banks and private banks. The private banks are relatively modern, but state banks are unionized and slow to introduce new technologies. No advertising is done in India per se, but public relations is used for media coverage. The Indian ad agency, Roger Perreira, is used to provide media exposure for Diebold's top executive visits to India. The agency does similar work for product exhibits. Public relations is also used in lieu of product advertising to build primary demand.

Diebold is a good example of a company that uses product modification. It essentially views the Indian market as in many ways similar to the way the U.S. market was in the early 1970s, particularly on the issue of customer trust in the ATM machine and in terms of product features.

Dana and TRW: Following the Market

Dana and TRW are suppliers of original and replacement automotive equipment. Both primarily serve the major vehicle manufacturers and assemblers in India, many of whom are prominent automobile multi-nationals. In the industrial market and aftermarket, Dana sells through distributors and to replacement stores. The major impetus to standardize for these two companies comes from their globalized multinational customers. This means that while TRW maintains the same identity around the world, it may have to make some modifications for the Indian market.

As one TRW executive puts it,

> The automotive business is becoming global, so customers we serve in India are in many ways the customers we serve here in the United States. Customers are taking a more global view in product development and are now manufacturing global platforms. So the cars that are made in India are basically the same design as cars that are made in Brazil or elsewhere. When TRW bids for, and wins a supply contract on that global platform, it commits to supply the requirements of that platform around the world. So in that sense, many product similarities are found. Obviously, the Indian market is smaller, still developing, and volume is lower and this impacts cost, pricing strategy, and profitability.

Owens Illinois: Material and Labor Issues

Owens Illinois is one of the largest makers of glass containers in India and, like many others interviewed for this study, markets to major food and beverage multinationals that entered India following the country's liberalization. Owens Illinois is attempting to standardize products worldwide, but is inhibited from doing so in India by the quality of materials and labor. The glass manufactured in India tends to be 40 percent heavier and of lower quality due to the nature of the raw materials. The country's underdeveloped distribution infrastructure inhibits standardization of marketing process.

Gillette: The Mass Market Approach

Gillette leans toward standardization in its products, but localizes advertising to some extent. As a Gillette executive puts it, "All of our products are the same. Where we do make modifications is in packaging. We try to reduce the pack size or we change the quality of the packaging material for cost."

Gillette aims to develop global franchises for its product by using a standardized approach. From a marketing perspective, the benefits of standardized programs are rationalized in the following terms by the Gillette executive:

> We are focused on leveraging the marketing development programs across a broad array of geographies, so the fixed costs in developing a product are spread over a much larger geographic base.

American Greetings: Changing the Culture

American Greetings entered the market using a licensing strategy, but it has trouble with a standardized approach in India because of the lower quality of paper and other raw materials used for greeting card production. Some of the unique features of the Indian market, in its view, require localization of both marketing program and process. The licensee in India handles all promotional aspects. Ironically, India has a sizable, English-speaking, middle-class population, but the habit of sending cards, which is a deep tradition in the English-speaking world, is missing in India. A high literacy rate is another leading indicator of potential number of cards sold, and India falls short on this as well. In essence, India does not have a culture of sending cards and assimilating greeting cards into another culture is not easy. As Peter Pizarro, Vice President, International Business Development at American Greetings puts it,

> Consumer non-durables like batteries, film, scotch-tape and razor blades can be sold in other countries with little modification, but

Ironically, India has a sizable, English-speaking, middle-class population, but the habit of sending cards, which is a deep tradition in the English-speaking world, is missing in India.

greeting cards are very culturally sensitive and need adaptation. The challenge in India is to develop primary demand, and this is difficult in a country with a low literacy rate, since card buying is a function of educational levels along with purchasing power. The price of a card is much lower in India (40 cents) and at this price, it is difficult to add additional value. The quality of the card is much lower, and the finish or extra value is not added due to the lower price point.

The amount of localization could change if a major retailer like Wal-Mart, whom American Greetings currently supplies, enters the Indian market. Wal-Mart's push for a standardized, better quality product may result in American Greetings using a wholly-owned subsidiary or joint venture to produce a higher quality card in India.

What Would Wendy's Do?

Wendy's, a fast-food multinational, has not entered India, but believes it would use a rather standardized product approach if it does enter the market in the future. Wendy's is strong on global branding and its positioning emphasizes high quality, variety, and restaurant atmosphere. Conceptually, it wishes to transfer this brand around the world. Factors favoring this approach are shrinking global communications and certain fundamental similarities inherent in frequent buyers of fast food around the world, such as a penchant for economy, convenience, filling and satisfying food, and a familiar and predictable eating experience. Moreover, the product satisfies a fundamental human need. However, Wendy's is quick to realize that while all four needs may be present in consumer segments across the globe, the ways in which these needs manifest themselves may be culturally dependent. For instance, the way in which "economy" is defined in India may be different because of differences in purchasing power and general economic conditions. These differences mean that some modification and product refinements may be necessary, but Wendy's overall strategy of using a standardized marketing program and process approach remains the same.

As a Wendy's spokesperson puts it, "We do not wish to compete with the local fast-food chains, but wish to give the consumer a genuine American fast-food experience." This approach, while harnessing the benefits of standardization could also serve to differentiate and position the Wendy's brand in a clearly marked niche that is not vulnerable to local competition.

High Technology Questions

Companies in the information technology industry in India seemed to use a high level of standardization in terms of product, if not in promotion. IBM, Hewlett Packard, and Xerox executives consistently noted that product modifications for India were minimal. A Hewlett Packard executive noted that its products sold in India are fairly standardized with minor modifications to suit local conditions. The printers sold in India, for instance, have to be modified not just to suit the voltage requirements, but also to suit the unreliable, fluctuating power supply, lower quality of paper, higher levels of dust, and temperature conditions. Yet, the company uses the same brand names and same ad slogans in India with some localization. In India, Xerox sells a product similar to the one sold in the U.S., with fewer features to accommodate the price sensitivity of the local consumer. Similarly, IBM markets a fairly standardized product in India with some modifications in promotion. An IBM executive interviewed seemed to capture the essential drivers of standardization for the IT companies:

> One of the factors very simply put is efficiency. The syndrome that says that we do not necessarily want to have the wheel reinvented here. Our fundamental objectives are to drive revenue and therefore, if you can standardize at substantial efficiency and cost savings, your speed to market can be improved.

Distribution, reported as a problem in India for most consumer durable and non-durable companies interviewed is not a major concern for IBM, Xerox, and Hewlett Packard, all of whom are currently operating there. This could be because most IT firms are recent entrants and, more importantly, the industry itself is of more recent vintage and the distribution has been set up from scratch.

Reasons for Standardization

These personal interviews provide some important insights regarding the U.S. global firms' approach to India. For most of the companies interviewed, standardization was driven by three primary motivations:

- First, to maintain a strong worldwide brand identity in the case of consumer goods companies. In many cases, they perceive the existence of similar cross-national consumer segments in the United States and in India and want to keep their global brand identity strong for these segments.

- Second, to follow their major multinational global customers into the market. This is especially true for business-to-business suppliers such as Dana, TRW and Owens Illinois.

- Third, to promote efficiency in product manufacture. This is especially true for the information technology firms which have to make only minor modifications for most new markets.

NOTES

1. Levitt, Theodore, "The Globalization of Markets," *Harvard Business Review*, May-June, 1983, 92-102.

2. Baker, James. C., John K. Ryans Jr., and Donald G. Howard, "Part VI, Exploring Global Markets," in *International Business Classics*, Boston: Lexington Books, 1988, 313-317.

CHAPTER 11

Promoting and Selling Products and Services

EARLIER discussions of entry strategy and market segmentation to reach the middle class have important implications for a firm's marketing strategies for India. For example, if the company enters via exporting and uses an Indian distributor, many decisions regarding promotion, advertising, pricing, and retail outlets will be made either in conjunction with, or independently by, its local representative. On the other hand, firms who choose to do much of their marketing themselves need to consider the best ways to reach their customers.

More frequently today, global companies are weighing questions like:

- Can I use the *same* (or similar) marketing strategies in India that I use elsewhere in the world?, and

- If I go totally *local*, what will it do to my marketing costs?

Typically, there are cost savings attached to using the same message and selling the same products in every market around the world. At the same time, making slight changes in its marketing approach may improve a company's position locally.

Marketing Services in India

Before we consider such questions, we need to learn more about the marketing services available in India. What kinds of media, marketing research firms, and advertising agencies are available in the major cities? Are retail outlets in India similar to those in the U.S., Canada, and Europe? What terms of sale and mark-ups are appropriate for India? Answers to these questions will indicate to what extent the use of a standardized marketing approach is an alternative here.

Media

Newspapers and magazines take the largest share of advertising expenditure in India—about 56 percent.

Fortunately, India is a media-rich country. Print and broadcast media are readily available in the major cities and, to a somewhat lesser extent, in rural areas. Let's look at each major media category to determine the possibilities.

Print

Newspapers and magazines take the largest share of advertising expenditure in India—about 56 percent. In the major cities, as well as in many regional centers, newspapers and magazines are widely available. Moreover, the educated Indian loves to read. According to the National Readership Survey (NRS), daily newspapers reach nearly two-thirds of urban adult Indians[1] and offer an excellent way to advertise consumer products. Similarly, a number of well-respected publications reach the business-to-business market.

The NRS Council includes representatives of the Indian Newspaper Society (INS), the Audit Bureau of Circulation (ABC) and Advertising Agencies Association (AAA). Each of these organizations represents important sources of information on Indian newspapers.

The largest English-language newspaper that provides access to 4.5 million Indians across the country is *The Times of India.* Owned by the Bennett Coleman Group, it is an important advertising vehicle to reach the middle- and upper-class segments. However, cities throughout the country are home to a wide range of regional and local newspapers.

Magazines are another significant print advertising medium in India, and there are excellent magazines targeting both the consumer and the business and trade markets. For example, we have often referred to *India Today,* an excellent example of a news magazine that is widely read by consumers, business leaders, and Non-Resident

Fake Brands: An Intellectual Property Concern

Illiteracy and the inability of many Indian shoppers to read English causes a major consumer products problem for multinational corporations. Since Procter & Gamble, Coca-Cola, Kellogg's, Unilever, Colgate-Palmolive, and most other foreign major brands are in English, this can create shopping problems for the bulk of Indian consumers. It also results in a large market for local Indian entrepreneurs, who deliberately produce bogus "look-alike" and "sound-alike" products.

Recognizing that such a large percentage of shoppers have difficulty with the English language, wily Indian entrepreneurs offer knock-off products. For example, one such local producer sells shampoo and soap using the labels "Head & Sholwers" and "Luk." Many unsuspecting consumers, intent on buying the well-known brand names "Head & Shoulders" and "Lux" become confused and are misled into buying the "look-alike" brands. This sort of problem occurs daily and affects a variety of MNCs who lose sales to the copycat brands.

How important is the fake brand problem? According to an article by *Bloomberg News* columnist Mrinalini Datta, P&G alone loses an estimated US$6.5 million a year due to such consumer confusion. And, not only does this fakery cost the various MNCs revenue, the poor quality of the look-alike brands can cause health problems and hurt the real brand's image.

Source: Mrinalini Datta, "India Is Awash in Copycat Brands,"
Cleveland Plain Dealer, September 6, 2000, p. C–1.

....

Indians via its U.S and Canadian editions. Among the general business population, *Business India* and *Business World* also have strong readership, as do a number of trade publications targeting specific industries. There are also a number of specialized consumer publications. For example, when Ford launched its Ikon in India, among the periodicals it used were those for car enthusiasts.

Television/Broadcast Media

According to NRS 2000 data, television reaches roughly three-fourths of all urban homes in India. Of special importance is the fact that satellite and cable television penetration is roughly 50 percent of all urban homes. The government-owned channel is Doordarshan and it has the potential to reach nine out of ten Indians. There are also a large number of satellite and cable channels from the West, including CNN, NBC, BBC, and Discovery, and all are available for advertising.

According to Gareth Chang, Chairman and CEO of Star TV, in India the company has expanded its management team and made one of its largest investments in the region in content. He says "China may have more luster to Western multinationals, but India is one of the world's largest democracies, has a larger middle class, and is more open than China, so it shouldn't be forgotten."[2] This reflects the continued growth in the broadcast media in India, including satellite TV, and the expected potential from advertising.

Advertising on radio is also possible. However, except for the government's All India Radio, the stations are all private FM music stations in a handful of cities, so the media buy is more fragmented. Radio gets only about 2 percent of advertising expenditure in India, compared with television's 36 percent.

Television ownership is one basis that might be used for market segmentation. Just over 30 percent of households overall own a television, with a much higher share in urban areas, as mentioned above. According to Kellogg's Managing Director in the Asia-Pacific area which includes India, the company's target customers are likely to have a TV. And, he says, if the households have a TV, they tend to have children as well. It is the households with children that represent the firm's target market and this is the reason why TV is a good medium for Kellogg's.

Movie Theaters

Cinema is extremely popular in India and movie attendance is high. Commercials shown in theaters provide a good, relatively inexpensive way to reach a large audience. This is also a medium that is effective in many rural areas and the smaller cities. As stated earlier, the popularity of the "Bollywood" stars makes them good potential product spokespersons. Currently, less than 1 percent of advertising expenditure in India goes to cinema, so commercials paired with movies are likely to get a lot of attention, especially with a youthful audience.

As in Europe, movie commercials are often the same as, or a somewhat longer version, of those shown on television. Of course, the format of the commercials must change for cinema showing. As in Europe, movie attendees tend to find the commercials entertaining. A relatively inexpensive commercial shown on a large screen to a "captive audience" can be very effective in promoting some consumer products.

Out-of-Home Advertising

About 6 percent of advertising expenditure in India goes to out-of-home media. Outdoor advertising can be used in India's major cities much as it is in the West and signage of various types can be found throughout the country. Especially noteworthy for many advertisers are the poster locations around the perimeter of the athletic fields. Cricket and soccer are two extremely popular sports in India and the signs surround the playing fields. Spectators rarely watch a match without being reminded of the products being advertised. The same can be said for TV viewers of the events. The April 23, 2001 issue of *India Today* had a two-page spread on the cricket series between India and Australia. A picture of the action on the field clearly showed a large Pepsi sign in the background.

Direct Mail

Direct mail is a viable promotional medium in India, especially for business-to-business. Census and voter records are allowed to be used. Telephone directories and auto-club lists are another source of prospect addresses. *The Handbook of International Direct Marketing* (4th edition) gives several examples of list costs. It cites a cost of about US$300 per thousand to reach 750,000 top executives of the largest companies or US$100 per thousand to reach 200,000 companies with sales of more than US$1 million, with industry selections possible. There are also lists of wealthy Indians, professionals, and board level executives.

Because English is the language of business and the common lan-

Direct mail is a viable promotional medium in India, especially for business-to-business.

A Unique "Direct Mail" Delivery System

In some major urban areas, newspapers are home delivered very efficiently during early morning hours. Newspaper vans deliver the newspapers in bundles to locations where home-delivery carriers separate them and carry them to the individual residences. In a variation on the newspaper inserts found in the U.S., a system has developed where these local carriers will, for a small fee, insert promotional materials in the newspapers that are delivered to the households. Thus, an advertiser can pre-select certain neighborhoods to receive its promotional materials. For example, a company could target its promotional materials to a select number of affluent neighborhoods in New Delhi. Since the inserts are included with the daily paper, which is widely read, the advertiser is assured that it will receive some attention from the selected households.

Source: Author interview.

guage in the country, direct mail in English is perfectly acceptable. The Indian postal service offers low prices but slow delivery that is sometimes unreliable. One option is to register mail; it takes longer for delivery but is much more reliable. Because of prohibitions on the import of many consumer goods, it is not safe to assume that orders from the United States could simply be delivered to a consumer in India. International courier services such as United Parcel Service and Federal Express do operate in India.

India has an active Direct Marketing Association with about 300 members. Contact information is in the sources section in the appendix. International companies are invited to use their services and become members.

Advertising Agencies

India has long had a reputation for having world class advertising agencies and its Advertising Agencies Association (AAA) is a strong player among the global advertising associations. Today, many of India's leading advertising agencies are partnered with the major global agencies, such as Saatchi & Saatchi, Dentsu, Ogilvy & Mather Worldwide, and

Foote, Cone, & Belding. Whenever a major merger of agencies in the U.S. or Europe occurs, this tends to have implications for the merged agencies' Indian partners. A recent example is the Leo Burnett and McManus Group merger in the U.S., which led ultimately to a merged entity in India called Starcom.

As might be expected, most large global companies operating in India are represented there by their global advertising agency or agencies. Thus, for example, Goodyear and Motorola were represented by McCann, Mars by D'Arcy, and Henkel by BBD&O, while Gillette was represented by BBD&O, McCann and O&M in 1999.[3] (Since advertisers often change agencies, their representatives may be different today.)

FIGURE 11. 1 ADVERTISING IN INDIA (2001)

Select global brands and their advertising agency

Agency	Global brands represented
Y&R Advertising Agency	United International Pictures, Merck, Revlon, Robert Bosch
BBD&O	Sony, FedEx, Visa, ICI Paints, Henkel
McCann-Erickson Worldwide	UPS, Unilever, Microsoft, Mastercard, ExxonMobil, GE (Lighting), GM
Euro RSCG Worldwide	Scherling Plough, Sara Lee, Unilever, Intel, GlaxoSmithKline
Ogilvy Mather Worldwide	Tricon, IBM, DHL Express, Gillette
Grey Worldwide	Wrigley, Unisys, Mars (petfood), Procter & Gamble, Oracle, Sony
Bates Worldwide	Hyundai, Pfizer, Allied Domeq
Saatchi & Saatchi	P&G, Transitions Optics
TBWA Worldwide	Samsonite, Vivendi, Briersdorf
FCB Worldwide	Sunkist, Samsung, Hilton Hotels, S.C. Johnson & Son
Publicis	Coca-Cola, Ericsson, Seimens, L'Oreal
J. Walter Thompson Co.	DeBeers, PepsiCo., Pfizer, Heinz, Kimberly-Clark, Nestlé, Kellogg's, Hallmark, Walt Disney, Royal Dutch Shell, Pillsbury
Lowe, Lintas and Partners Worldwide	Unilever, Eastman Kodak, Johnson and Johnson, Nestlé
D'Arcy	Embraer, Mars
DDB Worldwide	McDonald's, Philips Electric
Bartle Bogle Hagarty	Reebok, Unilever
The Batey Group	Singapore Airlines

Source: Conor Dignam, "Connecting the Dots," *adageglobal,* September 2001, pp. 24-35.

Award-Winning Advertising People

It certainly is not unusual for Indian advertising people to win international awards. In June 2001, *adageglobal* picked the top 100 Directors (worldwide) for TV advertising. Among the top 100 was India's Prasoon Pandey. He has made more than 100 commercials and in 1995, he received India's "Director of the Year" award. Pandey has received national and international awards for commercials for advertisers, including Ericsson Mobile Phones, *The Times of India* and Bajaj Auto. Such awards indicate the high quality of the advertising industry in the country.

Source: "Top 100 Directors," *adageglobal,* June 2001, p. 6.

....

Even as the various Asian markets began to recover from their year 2000 economic problems, most major global network agencies showed increased billings and gross income. The U.S. recession in late 2001 had some impact on the region, but less than expected.

In a study of major global agencies published by *adageglobal* in 2001, India ranked fifth in Asia in both agency income increase and total billings.[4] In fact, the major agencies in India showed a 21 percent total increase in gross income and a 17.9 percent increase in total billings. As might be expected, Japan ranked first in Asia, but India's performance placed it ahead of such expanding markets as Taiwan, Singapore, and Thailand.

Advertising Leaders

According to *adageglobal,* the leading international advertising publication, Unilever was the top advertiser in India in 2000 with an expenditure topping US$240 million.[5] After Unilever, the total expenditure for the remaining "top 10" advertisers in India drops sharply. Second ranking was held by P&G with more than US$74 million, while a local company, Paras Pharma, ranked third with about US$57 million. Other members of the "top 10" included (in order) Colgate-Palmolive Co., PepsiCo, Dabur India, Coca-Cola Co., BPL India, Nestlé, and Godrej Soaps.

Unilever, which owns majority control of Hindustan Lever, its Indian operation, is one of the few foreign consumer goods manufacturers that has a major presence in rural India. It has an estimated 70 percent market share for low-cost soaps and skin care products.[6] It has turned more attention to its upscale Lakme products and tailors some marketing messages to the high- and middle-income markets with commercials on MTV India and other channels. In rural India, it may send theater troupes to villages, stick gold coins in soap bars, and use other innovative methods.[7] Lever has annually spent a large advertising budget over the years, and it clearly has been rewarded in terms of market share and brand recognition.

While the focus here appears to be on the global giants of the advertising world, (i.e. MNCs and agency "giants"), India has many advertising agencies throughout the country. A good source of information on local agencies is the Advertising Agencies Association (AAA). The address of the AAA is included in the appendix.

Marketing Research

As with the global advertising agencies, some of the leading U.S. and other Western marketing research firms have set up operations in India. For example, A.C. Nielsen International Research, the world's largest marketing research firm, has an extensive presence there. Similarly, the Blackstone Group, Chicago, has partner research offices in Mumbai, Delhi, Bangalore, Kolkata, Chennai, Hyderabad, and Cochin.[8] Among the other firms listed by *Marketing News* as having Indian operations were: Audits & Surveys Worldwide, CLT International, Customer Satisfaction Management and Measurement, Market Probe, Inc., SIS International Research, and Walker Information.

ESOMAR, the world association for marketing research professionals, based in the Netherlands, has 10 member companies from India who are considered major players in marketing research. Firms like the Indian Market Research Bureau offer several syndicated surveys as well as custom research. It conducts national readership surveys, television ratings, a survey of business people, and omnibus studies on medical products and doctors, and on business travelers. It has 13 field offices, and 5 full-service offices and is headquartered in Mumbai. Most national market research firms in India have some international affiliation.

In terms of total market research expenditures, India ranked seventh in the Asia-Pacific region in 1999 with an estimated total of US$46.9 million, excluding in-house marketing research. Figure 11.2 below shows country-by-country data for the region.

FIGURE 11.2 MARKETING RESEARCH IN THE ASIA PACIFIC REGION,[10] 1999

Country	Spending on market research in US$ millions	
Japan	$1062.2	
Australia	283.4	
China	133.2	
Korea	75.6	
New Zealand	59.7	
Hong Kong (China)	55.4	
India	46.9	
Taiwan	40.5	*Source: Marketing News.*

Distribution

India's sheer geographic size and its transportation inadequacies make nationwide distribution a formidable task. Couple these concerns with a retailing structure that lacks any comprehensive retailer, like a Wal-Mart or Carrefour, and the challenge becomes even clearer. Therefore, it is not surprising that Hindustan Lever has received kudos for its distribution system that reaches 70,000 villages where 40 percent of the rural population lives.[10]

Presently, most U.S. and Canadian firms are not concerned with reaching "everyone" in India, but rather with reaching the key larger markets. As mentioned earlier, India's six primary cities contain the bulk of the middle and upper income markets and for business-to-business firms, the majority of the manufacturers. Further these areas tend to have a significant number of agents, distributors, and wholesalers.

According to the U.S. Department of Commerce office in India, when a company wants to sell its products or services in India before establishing a branch office or a subsidiary, it can enter the market by appointing an agent or a distributor. If the product has a wider or specialized market, it would be appropriate to appoint agents regionally.

With the gradual opening up of the market in line with India's WTO commitments, U.S. exporters will find a high response rate from potential agents and distributors for many products. At first glance, many agents appear to have excellent industry and customer contacts. They will have typically developed and nurtured these contacts over time, and their primary interest in a distributorship is to sell to these contacts. These agents may have little motivation to develop new markets or new customers. It is important to gauge your prospective agents' aggressiveness in developing new networks and contacts.

Most Indian manufacturers use a three-tier selling and distribution structure that has evolved over the years: distributor, wholesaler, and retailer. A company operating on an all-India basis could have between 400 and 2,300 distributors. The retailers served directly by a company's distributors may similarly be between 250,000 and 750,000. Depending on how a company chooses to manage and supervise these relationships, its sales staff could vary from 75 to 500 in number.

Typical gross margins for a distributor, wholesaler, and retailer are 4-5, 3-4, and 10-15 percent, respectively. Wholesaling is profitable by maintaining low costs and high turnover. Many wholesalers operate out of wholesale markets. India has approximately 4 million retailers, mostly family-owned or family-run businesses. In urban areas, the more enterprising retailers provide credit and home delivery.

In recent years, there has been increased interest by companies in improving their distribution logistics in an effort to address a fiercely competitive market. This in turn has led to the emergence of independent distribution and logistics agencies to handle this important function. Marketers are increasingly outsourcing some of the key functions in the distribution and logistics areas, and looking for more and better options to reach the consumer. Most fast moving consumer goods *Continues page 126*

In India, familiarity breeds better content

By Melissa LeHardy and Amy Ryan

As more companies expand their target markets to include customers in other countries, international marketing research has become an increasingly important step in ensuring successful product development and rollout. With more than 5 million PCs installed nationwide and reportedly, some 5.5 million Internet users, India is the international market's newest technology consumer powerhouse.

As this region develops, global IT marketers are wise to add respondents from this country to their research agenda, but differences in culture and infrastructure must be noted and respected. Marketers must plan accordingly before beginning any research in this region to make sure the differences do not become stumbling blocks to a marketing program.

Conducting research in India, as in all distant geographies, means an extensive checklist to help guarantee a seamless project schedule. Planning the project carefully and understanding India's unique culture—most notably, the nation's stratified society, developing infrastructure and multiple languages—will help researchers collect the most useful marketing data.

Because of traditions held with regards to class, gender and age, qualitative focus groups in India are typically designed with as much homogeneity as possible, which helps the participants feel comfortable and lends itself to gathering the most useful responses. Differences in social status, education levels, age or gender can make participants uncomfortable, so one respondent type per session is the rule.

While telephone and online research methods are widely used in most quantitative studies in the United States and Europe, India's developing communications infrastructure makes in-person interviewing the most effective way to collect information—in fact, 95 percent of quantitative research now is conducted this way. Furthermore, interviewers rarely have the luxury of bringing respondents to a central location to complete the survey and instead must go to the respondent's office or home.

Selecting local moderators and interviewers familiar with several Indian dialects is a must. Indians speak in more than 16 distinct languages, and the moderators must be fluent in the language selected for the group or interview. In addition, project leaders must make sure each respondent is fluent in the selected language or dialect. Even if English is the language selected for the research, local moderators will bring to the sessions an understanding of local customs and practices, an awareness of any regional laws governing marketing research practices, and a familiarity with the local economy and relevant news and events.

When conducting research in real time, choose a simultaneous translator completely fluent in the language selected for the sessions as well as in English as you will want to have a complete understanding of all the responses. As with all foreign language groups and interviews, carefully observe the participants' body language and gestures while listening to the voice-over.

Unlike in more developed countries with multiple facilities designed specifically for marketing research studies, most research in India is held in spaces that are most comfortable for the participants, which in turn provides for more honest responses. A focus group or interview among housewives most likely will be held at a home matching the participants' socioeconomic backgrounds. Conversely, a business to business focus group or interview among men may be held at a hotel or office.

Remember that to successfully include India in a research program, marketers must be culturally literate and ready to address the many issues that will present themselves while working with this diverse population. Come prepared with knowledge of what makes the country unique, and not only will you obtain valuable marketing data, you will come away with a greater appreciation for Indian culture.

This article originally appeared in *Marketing News* on April 23, 2001 and appears here with permission. © Marketing News, 2001. Ms. LeHardy and Ms. Ryan work for Answers Research, Inc., a California-based marketing research firm.

(FMCG) and pharmaceutical companies use Clearing and Forwarding (C&F) agents for their distribution and each C&F agent services stock lists in an area, typically a state. It is also important to note that duty structures vary across different states for the same product, thus creating disparate pricing. With the cost of establishing warehouses becoming extremely high, C&F agents are fast becoming the norm for the future. Recent years have also seen innovative trends by companies in using distribution channels for products with synergy.

India, in recent times, has also seen the emergence of mature channels of distribution and support for products such as computer hardware, software, and peripherals ranging from commodity product to high-end IT equipment. The typical distribution structure has been two-tiered with one distributor (for the entire country) servicing dealers and retailers.

For most newcomers to India, the use of distributors, agents or wholesalers represents the level of commitment they desire at the outset. However, another possibility for firms desiring a strong immediate presence involves entering into a joint venture with a local Indian producer. A joint venture can provide an immediate distribution structure, as of course, can an acquisition. (As noted in an earlier chapter, the opportunity for majority control/acquisitions is now a possibility in many sectors that have been deregulated.) Care should be taken when entering a distribution agreement. The U.S. Department of Commerce offices in New Delhi and six other Indian locations can be extremely helpful in the screening process, as well as helping to identify prospective agents, and distributors. In fact, by contacting one of the U.S. Department of Commerce offices throughout the U.S., a firm can take advantage of the Agency Distributor Service (ADS).

Retailing

By Western standards, the retail distribution system in India is relatively underdeveloped and antiquated. U.S., Canada, Europe, and the major South American countries, for example, can be characterized as having now moved (or begun to move) from the large department store/supermarket/global specialty store era to the hypermarket era. The Wal-Marts and Carrefours have developed a strong presence in the EU and NAFTA countries as well as Chile, Brazil, Argentina, and beyond. Further, China has begun to see the entry of the hypermarket, as have other Asian markets. At the same time, these same countries have seen the continued growth of specialty shops, particularly the high-end specialty shops. India, however, has not reached the stage of having major stores and supermarkets, much less the hypermarket stage.

As Neelam Mathews wrote in *Chain Store Age,* "India is particularly raw territory for retail chain stores though they have become more prevalent in the last four years."[11] Reportedly, many major retailers, including Wal-Mart, have looked at India in recent years, but have not entered. The head of Kurt Salmon Associates' Technopak, suggests that the absence of large chains can be attributed to time-consuming challenges posed by logistics.[12] Three other reasons cited for the limited interest on the part of big retailers are the lack of a branding culture, the cost of real estate, and the failure of financial institutions to lend to retailers.

KSA Technopak predicts that retail sales in India will grow to US$220 billion in 2002, and to reach US$270 billion by 2005. In contrast, an A. T. Kearney study reported in the same article sets the 2005 projection at US$350 billion.[13]

While the large chains are still watching India, but seem reluctant to act, several U.S. specialty store groups have entered the country. Levi Strauss and Liz Claiborne are examples of Western brand leaders establishing multiple shops in the country. And, a number of clothiers have plans to open exclusive shops in India. For more insight into the opportunities in the retail sector, see the article in the appendix from *The McKinsey Quarterly,* pp. 165.

Franchising

A number of U.S. companies that operate through franchises are found in India. These include McDonald's, Pizza Hut, Dunkin' Donuts, KFC, Budget, Hertz, and Best Western.

The Franchising Association of India (FAI) was established in 1999 through the efforts of the Indo-American Chamber of Commerce and it is a member of the World Franchising Council. The FAI can provide information to U.S. firms interested in establishing franchises in India, including the identification of potential Indian franchisees.

Many companies with franchises in India have found it to be a good market for their products and services. To date, most are operating in the major cities, such as New Delhi and Mumbai.

Direct Selling

A rapidly growing form of marketing in India is direct selling. A number of U.S. and foreign firms, such as Avon, Amway, Hindustan Lever, Tupperware, and Aero Pharma are currently engaged in direct selling. It has been estimated by the Indian Direct Selling Association (IDSA) that the industry employed 700,000 sales people in 2001 and the number is increasing annually. Clearly, this is a relatively low cost way of selling and distributing products in India.

With the growing unemployment and underemployment due to government privatization efforts, the numbers of available workers for direct selling is increasing. For more information on the use of direct selling, contact the IDSA or the U.S. Department of Commerce in India.

NOTES

1. DOC 2000 report reporting on National Readership Survey.
2. Madden, Normandy, "Experts pick key emerging markets for 2000: China, India, Poland," *Advertising Age International*, February 2000, p. 26.
3. Dietrich, Joy, "World Brands," *Advertising Age International*, September 1999, pp. 29–44.
4. Madden, Normandy, "Asia Back on Top," *adageglobal*, August 1, 2001, p. 15.
5. "The World's Marketing Elite by Country," *adageglobal*, November 2001, p. 36.

6. Merchant, Khozem, "Striving for Success—One Sachet at a Time," *Financial Times,* December 11, 2000, p. 9.

7. Tanzer, Andrew and Chandrani Ghosh, "Soap Opera in India," *Forbes,* June 11, 2001, pp. 129–130.

8. "2001 Directory of International Research Firms," *Marketing News,* April 23, 2001, pp. 18–19.

9. ESOMAR Statistics, *Marketing News,* July 2, 2001, p. 15.

10. Merchant, Khozem, "Striving for Success—One Sachet at a Time," *Financial Times,* December 11, 2000, p. 1.

11. Mathews, Neelam, "India's Retail Rush," *Chain Store Age,* August 1999, p. 52.

12. *Op. cit.*

13. *Op. cit.*

CHAPTER 12

The Services Economy in India:
A Dynamic Sector

AS A developing country, one would expect the Indian economy to be largely an agrarian economy and agriculture is certainly a major part of India's GNP. It is also a labor-intensive activity. However, agriculture has slipped from the earliest days of the Indian Republic when it contributed 55.4 percent of the national income compared with 25.5 percent today.

A surprising feature of the Indian economy is the dynamic services sector. According to government data, services accounted for 52.4 percent of the national income in the fiscal year 1999–2000 compared with 31.8 percent in the 1950s. Manufacturing contributes 22.1 percent today, compared with 12.8 percent in the 1950s.

In the export sector, the major growth in recent years has been in the area of software services offered both on site and offshore.

In the export sector, the major growth in recent years has been in the area of software services offered both on site and offshore. Currently, software exports are at about US$4 billion and the government has ambitious targets of software exports of US$50 billion or more by 2010. In this section we look at the services sector of the Indian economy and assess its status and possible future direction.

The services sector has been growing in India more rapidly than in advanced western economies and now it is estimated that one in every two people is employed in the services industry. Services encompass a wide range of offerings and are also becoming a career choice for many professionals. This means that the economy has moved from a base in agriculture to a base in services while manufacturing has lagged. This may well be considered a weak point in comparison with China, which has attracted massive amounts of manufacturing investment from all over the world.

Part of the growth in the services sector can be explained by the liberalization of the Indian economy. Unlike manufacturing, historically either a public sector "business," or a *license raj* protected by the government, many newer industries have been open to private interests from the beginning. Two examples are cable TV and cellular telephony.

The Services Economy and Its Subsectors

Retailing

India has one of the most underdeveloped retail sectors in the world. This is explained in part by the fact that retailing was historically a mom and pop dominated sector and it was accorded a lower status in India's caste system. As a consequence, organized retailing with an emphasis on self-service and chain stores that can achieve system-wide economies are a recent entry to the Indian retailing scene. In some of the more affluent sections of major Indian cities, one can now find multiunit supermarket chains catering to the middle and upper classes with packaged foods and other consumer products.

The exact size of the organized sector of the Indian retailing sector and its share of the overall retail sector is difficult to assess. The unorganized sector still dominates and includes the inevitable component of the underground economy. However, the total retail industry is estimated to be about US$50 billion and one would expect that with greater affluence and increasing time pressures on dual-income couples, the sector will grow faster than in the past.

Financial Services Including Banking and Insurance

This is another example of a sector that has been long dormant because it was largely controlled and heavily regulated by the government. Major international banking firms such as Citibank, Standard Char-

Growing insurance sector comes with privatization

While the banking and stock market communities in India have had many problems, the newly privatized insurance sector has attracted many of that industry's global leaders. New York Life International, Sun Life, AIG, Prudential, and Standard Life are among the eleven global companies that received licenses from India's Insurance Regulatory and Development Authority (IRDA) between August 2000 and May 2001. Prior to the opening of the insurance sector, two state run insurers controlled the industry and only 10 percent of the Indian population had life insurance. However, the insurable population is estimated at 15 to 25 percent. One of the entrants already has 500 agents in the country.

Source: Angus Donald, "Market Opens Up," *Financial Times,* May 8, 2001, p. VI.

....

tered, and Hong Kong and Shanghai Bank have operated in India for many decades, but their main role has been to provide merchant banking services to multinational and Indian firms. They have had minimal exposure to the retail banking sector which has been dominated by "nationalized" banks. The State Bank of India continues to be the largest retail bank with more branches than any other bank in the world. A unionized work force, which has often resisted any attempts at automation and greater efficiency, has meant that the banking sector has been slow to change.

Only recently has the Indian legislature passed laws designed to allow the entry of foreign insurance firms.

A similar situation has occurred in the insurance sector where one large state-sanctioned company, the Life Insurance Corporation of India, has dominated the scene. Only recently has the Indian legislature passed laws designed to allow the entry of foreign insurance firms. Within the next few years, more change is expected to occur in this sector than has been the case in the previous hundred!

As for other financial services, the Indian market has been opening slowly. Several foreign investment funds and mutual funds have entered the market, but they are still mostly restricted to domestic investment opportunities. One reason is the nonconvertibility of the rupee as noted by Rajiv Vij, Head of Franklin Templeton Fund in India during an interview with the authors. Periodic high profile incidents such as the stock market scam of several years ago, and the more recent problems faced by India's premiere home-grown investment institution, Unit Trust of India, make for continuing uncertainty in the financial services sector, generally. But, as Mr. Vij noted, the trend towards liberalization of the Indian economy, overall, and in the financial services sector in particular, is expected to continue.

India's economy is still, for the most part, a cash economy. A small segment of the population does carry credit cards, but it will be some-time before any significant consumer credit economy will develop. A similar observation applies to the area of housing and mortgage finance even though one of the most successful and innovative firms in the Indian financial services industry in recent years has been the quasi-private Housing Development and Finance Corporation. Whatever the uncertainties in the short term and the periodic "shocks" experienced by the sector, those who are in it for the long haul should be able to look forward to significant opportunities over the coming decade and beyond.

Transportation

In many respects, the transportation sector has some of the most intractable problems in the Indian economy, but at the same time, it is the sector that will be crucial to economic success in coming years. Each of the three modes of transportation is plagued by the very poor state of infrastructure that requires massive levels of investment for modernization. The areas in need are railways, roadways, and airports.

Railways: The Indian railway system is one of the oldest and most extensive in the world. Given the vast geographic expanse of India, rail is the only viable means of transportation for the great majority of Indian passengers both in terms of availability and affordability. *McKinsey Quarterly* reports that the Indian railways are by far the largest passenger railway system in the world. In 1998, the railways

Private sector Indian bank's major purchase of ATMs

In a July 25, 2001 press release, Diebold HMA Private Limited announced the largest single Indian order for automated teller machines. The order from UTI Bank called for a minimum of 300 ATMs. UTI Bank, founded in 1994, is one of the first private banks established in India. The purchase indicates its desire to introduce state-of-the-art technology in the banking sector. Diebold HMA Private Limited is a joint venture between Canton, Ohio's Diebold Inc. and HMA Data Systems (India). UTI has 88 full service branches nationwide and has the nation's second largest ATM network.

Source: Diebold Press Release Internal Announcement, July 25, 2001.

....

clocked 380 billion passenger kilometers. They are ahead of China by 3 percent and ahead of Japan, the next highest country, by fully 50 percent. On the freight side, India is fourth at 284 billion freight-tonne kilometers, ranking behind China, the Russian Federation, and Burlington Northern of the United States.

The Indian railway system was established in the mid-nineteenth century and today employs over 1.5 million people. It covers a 62,000-kilometer route with 80,000 kilometers of track of which fully one-fifth has been converted to electric traction. Historically, the railways have been subdivided into about ten divisions in order to facilitate administration. A separate ministry of the Indian central government oversees the functioning of the railway system. Each Spring the minister in charge of railways presents a railway budget at about the same time as the minister in charge of finance presents the national budget. The whole country follows this budget because it establishes tariffs for both freight, which interests business people, and for passengers, which is important for the over 10 million passengers who travel by rail each year.

The challenge facing the Indian railway system is the same one that confronts all infrastructure sectors in the country—finding the investment to keep an aging system operating in terms of track and rolling stock. The railways have advanced in computerization of the passenger reservation system and the conversion of traction to both electric and diesel, but the demands on the system are so great that massive new investment will still be needed. In a poor country, tariff increases cannot fund investment in infrastructure. Privatization is also an unlikely solution in the railway sector because of the size of its unionized workforce and the lack of success in other countries in privatizing railroads, especially passenger lines.

Roadways: Compared with the railway network, the road network in India is underdeveloped and this greatly impacts the speed with which passengers or freight can be moved by road. As a consequence, most distribution by truck takes place only on an intra-state or regional basis. Both state-owned highways and private road operators coexist in most parts of the country. A system of limited access, long distance highways is imperative if road transport is ever to become economically efficient. As with the railways, the investment needed for any large scale development of highways has to be raised from international development and other multilateral agencies which would still look for an economic basis for justifying such investment.

Airways: The airline industry in India has been largely state-owned, and given the high cost of air travel, much of the population does not have access to this mode of transportation. It has also not been a major mode of transport for freight given the relatively small industrial sector and the dominance of basic industry, which lends itself more to rail and road transportation. In the past decade, some limited competition has been introduced in the domestic airline sector with the emergence of a handful of private airlines. Many of these, including a partnership between the Indian business group of Modi and the German airline Lufthansa, did not operate for long. The major domestic airline, Indian Airlines, is state-owned. As this book went to press, Jet Airways, a comparatively large domestic airline with connections to many cities, was the only private airline of any size operating in India. While the private efforts have improved service and provided competition to Indian Airlines, there has been little effect on price competition.

On the international side, the only Indian airline operating is Air India, although Indian Airlines also has limited service to a few international destinations within the region. While it has been profitable in some years, Air India has found it difficult to compete with major international airlines. As part of its less-than-enthusiastic moves toward privatization, the Indian government has often talked about partial privatization of both Indian Airlines and Air India. It is not clear, however, that there would be an overwhelming response to part ownership of the airlines among foreign investors or airline companies. For the moment, the airline industry in India is a question mark. It also is affected by infrastructure problems with poor airport facilities and a primitive level of ground services.

This sector's future rests on the overall performance and growth rate of the Indian economy, as well as the ability of the Indian government to administer the bitter medicine of full privatization. Simultaneously it must find the investment needed to upgrade the airport and other infrastructure to minimal international transportation standards.

CHAPTER 13

Speaking from Experience: Hewlett-Packard (HP India)

This case study is based upon an interview with Mr. Mohan Garde, vice president of business development on March 6, 2001.

Background

HP is a big company organized by businesses. In India, the business is divided into two parts: consumer business, and commercial and enterprise business. My background and experience are in the consumer business, so the context I will give is in the consumer business, rather than the commercial and enterprise business.

Our consumer business in India includes PCs and printers. We have two managers there, one for the commercial and enterprise side and one for the consumer business.

We started in India about 30 years ago with a calculator business handled initially by a distributorship called Blue Star. We then moved to a new business model by sending a country manager to set up an office in India and be responsible for the overall HP business there. About 10 years ago, we formally created HP India, a wholly owned subsidiary. Organizationally, it works like any other entity, but legally it is HP India.

Political System

India is a big democracy. In my mind, the system itself is similar to the U.S., but there is a difference in the number of industries regulated by the government, either through tariffs or through licenses that were awarded to people for privileged products. In our industry, the licenses have never been an issue. Tariffs are more of a problem. Now they are 35 to 40 percent on the types of imported consumer products that HP makes. For a while, there was a 100 percent tariff on these kinds of products. Tariffs are coming down every year, but they are still in the neighborhood of 30 percent. That means any domestic computer manufacturer has a 30 percent advantage, because they are not importing. However, if they are importing components, so they do not have that much of an advantage.

Familiarity with Free Enterprise

India's computer industry is largely free enterprise. Government does not interfere, so the key difference is that PC builders in India are largely fragmented "screw driver shops" that assemble PCs. Most branded PCs are made by foreign companies. So, in the PC industry in India there are many little companies, compared with a few major brands in the U.S.

Size of Middle Class

This depends on the definition of the middle class. The big difference is that in the U.S. most of the middle class have already adopted computing technology. In 60 percent of U.S. households that already have PCs, these products are affordable. So, if you are in this 60 percent you are definitely in the middle class in the U.S. The issue is different in India where the PC penetration has been at the very highest income levels. The size of that group is significant, but recently many in India have started purchasing PCs, since incomes have gone up and prices have come down.

Distribution System

The big difference I see in the distribution system is that about 10 retailers in the U.S. dominate the PC and consumer electronics business, whereas in India there is a two-tier system. Here in the U.S., we sell to retailers and they sell to consumers. In India, a wholesaler sells to a small retailer who sells to the consumer. The more you are in contact with the person you are selling, the more you can work with them directly.

Competitive Environment

HP has the highest market share in India so the competitive environment is not as intense for us. The local competition is not that strong.

Management Style

I think they are becoming very professional. Businesses are no longer family run, homegrown businesses. They are run by professional managers.

Marketing to the Middle Class

Most of our businesses are high volume, low margin kind of businesses, such as printers and PCs, compared with a digital TV set, which is low volume and high margin. It used to be that products with older technology were sold in the Asian markets, but that has changed now. In India, consumers want the latest technology.

In a city like Bangalore, every householder in an area like Coramangala is a target customer. They all have PCs because they are affluent enough to buy PCs for their children's education. When we sold PCs earlier, our market was the high-end consumer, but now we are targeting a broader market and are not limited to a narrow slice at the upper end.

At the high end I would say the market is very similar to the U.S. At the mid-range there is a big difference since there is a big impact of price and value. Everything in India is value-oriented, they do want good quality, but if you look at the product line there is a skew towards the lower end of the offering as compared with the high end of the offering. People do not want to pay much for the frills.

Historically, given the low penetration rate of PCs in the home, we have done category-based marketing, not segment-based marketing. We sell PCs, so we have a marketing program for PCs. Yes, the ad may be geared towards people in the high-income level, but we do not really say let's go to the middle class and market to them. It may be the promotion is geared in such a manner, around education perhaps, as to reach people who want to buy PCs for their children's education. In general, marketing geared to segments like the middle class is done for very high mass market products, like Coke or Pepsi. People buy our products, which are fairly expensive, after research. It is not an impulse purchase. So, it is the brand and quality that matters more than lifestyle associations.

Marketing and Advertising

Basically we have one brand everywhere. In India we sell under the HP name. Every product that we make is branded as an HP PC. The ad slogan "HP Invent," carries through everywhere and it is the same. The basic themes for media of how we want to build our brand and how we want to make our spending are set centrally. Execution is local. Increasingly, we have been trying to make regional ads. We may choose an ad and use different talent and voiceovers and so on, but it is the same theme. It may have Indians featured in the ad in India and Malaysians featured in the ad in Malaysia, but TV ads are done all together. We do not do that much TV advertising. Print advertising is developed locally, again with the main messages and ideas the same, but with ad copy developed locally.

We do not run pre- and post-tests in India due to time and money constraints. The other difference is in India we take an advertisement to market and learn from it and improve it the next time instead of pre-testing.

Standardization of Product

Our product is fairly standardized with some minor modifications. I will give some examples:

Power supply. Power in India is more unreliable, voltage fluctuates more. The power supply in most of our products is external to the device itself. It is like a wire with a little adapter which plugs into your wall. So we make sure that this power supply is qualified for operating conditions.

Paper jams. Quality of paper varies significantly. We want to make sure that because of the lower quality of paper used in India, our printers do not jam paper. We have modified the paper mechanism, so it is more tolerant towards paper which is rougher.

Dust. In the U.S. our products usually operate in air-conditioned, or protected environments. In India, and most emerging markets, there tends to be more temperature variation and there is more dust in the environment. Our product is an electro-mechanical device and dust can get inside and damage it. So, sometimes we have designed or made minor modifications in the printer to prevent these problems.

Heavier use. Another example is that the use of the product in India tends to be much higher because it is shared more. Using it at five times the duty cycle is common in India, where a personal printer becomes a departmental printer with eight people using it. So the duty cycle becomes high and sometimes this leads to quality problems because the product is not designed to run so many pages through it.

Repair vs. replace. In India, people tend to repair things more, whereas in the U.S. we replace them.

Dealer's role. Here you go to CompUSA and buy the product and take it home and it's your problem to set it up. In India, the dealer comes to your house to set it up for you.

Cultural Differences

There is a big cultural difference between the two markets, but we are not doing lifestyle marketing, so it does not really make much of a difference to us. Obviously, you want to avoid some of the common pitfalls such as using words incorrectly. For example, creativity might be highly valued in the U.S. Many people spend time doing creative things with PCs such as photography and design. It has not evolved to that extent in India, so the difference may be cultural or just a matter of time and purchasing power. The PC in India is purchased for a very specific purpose, such as children's education and not for photography.

How do these perceptions affect standardization? Actually, our product is standardized. We do a few things differently, but essentially our main product does not need to be localized. If a product comes bundled with software, we make the decision locally as to the software bundle. The wrapper and the "soft stuff" may be localized, but what you want to do in any big company is to standardize the core product itself in order to drive economies of scale. As for elements that need to be differentiated or do not lend themselves to economies of scale, you want to do them locally.

CHAPTER 14
Information Technology: Engine of Growth?

"From a distance, India often appears as a kaleidoscope of competing, perhaps superficial images. . . . The truth is no single image can do justice to your great nation."

—Bill Clinton, speech on visit to India in March 2000.

"India is a developing country with a developed-country R&D infrastructure."

—Jack Welch, former CEO, General Electric

IN THE quotes above, the former U.S. president and Jack Welch are responding to the paradox of change and development in India. It is still a developing country mired in developmental problems of poverty and illiteracy, yet it has a nuclear arsenal and the world's second largest pool of skilled software talent after the United States. During his visit to India in March 2000, the first by a U.S. president in over two decades, Clinton applauded India's achievements in science and technology, while calling for cooperation in commerce and the emerging knowledge-based industries.[1] The business purpose of Clinton's visit was three-fold:

1. To promote free trade with the new and growing India,

2. To advance U.S. business interests in having access to India's human resource capability, and

3. To help develop India as a new market for U.S. information technology (IT) interests.

The historic visit drew the world's attention to India's advantage in information-related high technology, innovation, and knowledge base, its large market, its well-developed R&D infrastructure, its large pool of cost-competitive technical talent, and the sophistication of Indian IT vendors. Most important, his visit helped pave the way for a mutually beneficial long term relationship between the two countries.

India has long been a forgotten nation when it comes to investment, largely due to its economic insularity stemming from its autarkic policies. The past decade, however, has been one of sea change for India. Catalyzed into breaking out of its insular mold by a balance-of-payments crisis in 1991, India is at last on the verge of freeing the tremendous potential that has been an inherent, yet untapped part of this sub-continent. India cannot match China in manufacturing prowess, economic growth, or its ability to attract foreign direct investment. However, it has discovered an untapped resource in its skilled work force, which is capable of powering the information technology revolution presently sweeping across the world. How the country uses this rich source of economic advantage will determine the country's economic fortunes as the century unfolds.

The disconnect between the talk by India's political elite of their country's becoming the next information technology superpower, and skeptical outsiders such as Jack Welch, former CEO of General Electric, could not be more stark. In a talk to Indian business people, Welch recognized India's "intellectual capital" and its sophisticated R&D infrastructure, while pointing out the old economic concerns such as lack of power generation capacity and a communications infrastructure that could hamper growth.[2] Welch's warning that India could fail to capitalize on the IT revolution, despite its prowess in software skills and R&D, should serve as a reality check for a country that is betting on IT to power its way into the new economy.

The information-based new economy requires a free business environment, unhampered by old economy regulations. In order to realize India's hopes for the IT sector, the government has to free the economy and allow economic and social change to transform the business climate. So far, the industry has succeeded against all odds and in spite of government inattention. If it is to maintain its projected and much vaunted growth, it needs to have a freer, more entrepreneurial climate that is friendly to new venture creation. It must offer easier access to capital markets and hard currency, set fewer bureaucratic and regulatory roadblocks, and provide better IT infrastructure such as reliable power and telecommunications.

India is at last on the verge of freeing the tremendous potential that has been an inherent, but untapped part of this sub-continent.

This section looks at the evolution of the IT industry in India. It includes an analysis of the projected potential of the IT, the role of industry organizations such as the National Association of Software and Service Companies (NASSCOM) in promoting the sector, and the role of government in facilitating the sector's growth. It concludes by profiling the top IT firms in India and their role in the industry's growth.

The software and information technology industry in India is without question one of the most dynamic sectors in India's economy. In 2001, it consisted of about 1000 companies employing 280,000 software engineers. The market capitalization of the firms in this sector was US$24.3 billion in September 1999.[3] According to NASSCOM, the revenues of the software industry in 1999–2000 were US$5.7 billion. Annual revenue for 2008 is projected to be around $87 billion. The industry has been growing at 50 percent annually since 1991. Worldwide, the sector is worth $850 billion with a projected growth of 50 to 60 percent per year. The Indian IT sector's growth since 1990 has been primarily export driven. In 1999, exports in this sector totaled US$4 billion and are projected to grow to US$50 billion by the year 2008. According to NASSCOM, 62 percent of the exports go to the United States, 23 percent to Europe, 4 percent to South East Asia, and 3.5 percent to Japan. The remaining 7.5 percent goes to West Asia, Australia, New Zealand, and the rest of the world.[4] A report by McKinsey Consulting projects that by 2008 Indian exports of software and services would account for 35 percent of all exports and 7.5 percent of GDP.

So far, the evolution of this sector has been incremental and organic in nature, but if it maintains its momentum and succeeds in realizing its potential, its impact on the economy and politics of India would be dramatic. Frankly, however, this is a big "if."

The IT sector in India came into the global limelight by the when an army of Indian software engineers were sent to foreign companies by Indian companies to write software code or to cure Y2K problems. Whereas margins from on-site work were necessarily low due to the high cost of transferring personnel to overseas locations, the Y2K work gave India an opportunity to showcase its IT capabilities on the international stage.

As it matures and migrates up the value ladder, the IT sector is gaining depth and sophistication in its portfolio of capabilities. This is reflected in the fact that cost is no longer the sole competitive tool for these companies. Their depth and diversification is beginning to allow them to compete on quality, speed, reliability, and innovation. Many Indian software companies are ISO 9001 certified and are able to offer world class services at competitive prices. As these companies move from value-based Y2K activities to value-added e-commerce work, their revenues are on the increase and the basis of competition is speed of delivery and faster cycle time, which supports a premium pricing strategy. The Indian IT industry shows signs of consolidation and growth through overseas acquisitions, both clear signs of maturity in the industry.

The offshore model (operations in India) is more profitable and helps India build its local infrastructure to support a strong and growing IT sector. The sector includes IT-enabled services, such as medical transcription, call centers, legal database work, logistics management, and web-content development, which are labor intensive and require IT skilled personnel. In fact, in many cases medical records for visits to U.S. physicians are transcribed in India. In the U.S., 200 out of the Fortune 500 now outsource this type of work to India. European companies do as well. It lets them take advantage of the low cost labor and the time-zone difference in India, which allows the U.S. or European firm to work on a 24-hour turnaround. As Indian firms move up the value ladder they are adding more value in services such as IT consulting, often from their overseas offices. Sometimes their ultimate goal is to develop branded software products designed for exports, but because marketing branded software in competitive overseas markets is capital intensive, this goal may be a long-term one.

Three broad characteristics define the new growth phase among the top players in India's IT industry: a foreign stock market listing, a global base of customers, and a multinational workforce.[5] The industry may be able to move up to branded product development if it maintains its current momentum.

PC Market in India

On the Indian domestic front, the hardware market is growing as domestic PC sales and sales of servers, printers, and notebook computers increase. PC penetration in India is currently quite low at 3.6 per 1000 population, compared with the U.S. at 363 per 1000. However, the buying power of India's formidable and growing middle class is substantial. Firms such as Hewlett Packard and IBM have entered the market focusing on this segment. As the interest in home Internet use increases along with the popularity of alternative Internet-access channels such as cybercafes in Indian cities, the potential for rapid growth in urban areas is real.

An article in one of India's leading newspapers, *The Hindu*, (November 8, 2000) claimed that PCs had become so important that people were opting for them over other consumer purchase goods and even taking loans to acquire them. Clearly, the key drivers of PC growth in India are Internet users who wish to enhance their computer skills and those who want to use it as a tool in children's studies. While PC prices are still relatively high, Indian households remain the fastest growing market for the PC manufacturers. In conversation with one of the authors, Mr. Ashok Benegal, general manager of Zenith Computers, an Indian firm, said that in early 2001, his company alone was selling about 200 PCs per day to the Indian household sector.

The increase in corporate users and the government's stated desire

An army of Indian software engineers were sent to foreign companies by Indian companies to write software code or to cure Y2K problems.

to move to incorporate computers in government are also important factors in increasing demand in the hardware market.

Role of States

Attracted by the infinite possibilities of growth and job creation offered by this sector, Indian states have been vying with each other to offer a hospitable environment for both foreign and domestic IT firms. E-governance has gained popularity in entrepreneurial states such as Andhra Pradesh, where the government has expressed a keen desire to leverage technology to spur development. The state's web site states its mission: "Andhra Pradesh will leverage Information Technology to attain a position of leadership and excellence in the information age and to transform itself into a knowledge society."[6] The governor of this state, dubbed the "laptop minister,"[7] has invested in a communications infrastructure to support e-governance. His efforts attracted Microsoft's product development center and GE Capital's international data center, which otherwise might have gone to the State of Karnataka. As India's first IT champion, the State of Karnataka now stands to lose that position as other states vie to attract foreign investors to their backyard by investing in the right infrastructure mix. Companies such as Microsoft cite better infrastructure as the primary reason for moving to Andhra Pradesh. The key cities of Bangalore (Karnataka State), Hyderabad (Andhra Pradesh), and Chennai (Tamil Nadu) in the south are referred to as the "silicon triangle" for having the highest concentration of IT industry in the country. Most of the World Bank's lending of $2 billion to India is concentrated on three states—Andhra Pradesh, Karnataka, and Uttar Pradesh. The reformist states in India are proving successful in attracting foreign investors as well as World Bank dollars to improve their infrastructure.

On the Indian domestic front, the hardware market is growing as domestic PC sales and sales of servers, printers and notebook computers increase.

Software Associations

The National Association of Software and Service Companies (NASSCOM) plays a pivotal role in the growth of the software category specifically and the IT sector, in general. The mission of NASSCOM is to be

IT Education in India

New world-class educational institutions are being set up in the more reformist-oriented states in India. During former President Bill Clinton's visit to India in March 2000, Motorola signed an agreement to set up Motorola School of Communication Technology at the Indian Institute of Information Technology (IIIT) in Hyderabad, one of the cities in the silicon triangle, and capital of the state of Andhra Pradesh. The Motorola School of Communication Technology is designed to be a state-of-the-art center for creating new talent by providing IT and telecom education. In addition, the school will offer research and development opportunities to innovate new approaches to wireless communications for the Indian Market (www.apit.com/iiitmou.html).

The Indian School of Business located in Hyderabad, brain child of Rajat Gupta, Managing Director of McKinsey and Co., is designed to provide business education in India. The school operates in collaboration with the Wharton School, University of Pennsylvania, and the Kellogg School of Business at Northwestern University. Both schools are supported and financed by leading companies in India and abroad, as well as the government.

As world class educational institutions enter and locate in India to satisfy the educational need, there will be more and better-educated information technology graduates. A reverse brain drain of Non-Resident Indians is spurring new entrepreneurial activity in the country and the energies of the local entrepreneurial talent are being unleashed by the government's willingness to provide incentives and relax regulatory controls for the IT sector. The government is finally facilitating the industry's growth, having realized that this may be the country's best chance to improve its economic fortunes and to achieve global integration and economic parity with the developed world in the long term.

Source: Author interview.

....

a one-stop provider of comprehensive information on all aspects of the software industry in India. As a non-profit organization, its goal is to facilitate India's emergence as a front runner in the information technology industry. The organization actively and effectively lobbies the government for improvements in IT infrastructure and changes in policy designed to promote the sector's growth. Its web site www.nasscom.org provides a gateway to the IT policies of the various states in India along with information on past and upcoming events in the IT sector and industry research and news. Its membership list includes most of the IT companies in India. It uses this information to match Indian companies with foreign IT companies and vice versa. As an industry promoter, NASSCOM is a key force for generating credibility in India's capability to participate fully in the global IT industry.

Capital Sources

A vibrant private sector to support entrepreneurial developments in the software and IT areas is growing in India. The expansion of this sector is helped by infusions of knowledge and capital from returning non-resident Indians (NRI) who are eager to share in the growth opportunities presented by the newly emerging IT sector.

Of late, venture capital activity has been growing in India. Foreign venture funds, some created by wealthy Indians based in the U.S. such as The Indus Entrepreneurs (TIE) and Chrysalis Fund have entered India seeking to invest in technology start-ups with good prospects for growth. Newer varieties of venture capitalists are also moving into India with foreign capital to fund Indian start-ups. A VC fund named At India, founded by a Silicon Valley NRI venture capitalist, calls itself a "business value accelerator" that seeks to provide value beyond capital. The venture capitalist has a joint venture with Silicon Valley–based Hambrecht & Quist and a venture capital base of US$50 million.[8] American firms with Indian subsidiaries, such as GE Capital and Intel, are investing in new ventures in India that have the potential to sell their products. As current restrictions on venture capital funds are eased by the government, more venture capital will be available to the IT sector. The sector will also benefit from changes in the availability of risk capital for entrepreneurial firms.

To summarize, the Indian IT industry's competitive advantage

Opportunities for women in high-tech India

Working outside the home is not new for Indian women. What is new is the quality and level of the positions they hold. High-tech industries are much less gender restrictive than other fields and industries. To illustrate, the National Association of Software and Service Companies reports that women are expected to be about 45 percent of the technical work force by 2010. It is not uncommon for women to have higher paying positions than their husbands, to have stock options, to travel alone for their jobs, and to hold top management positions in firms. This is a far cry from the arranged marriages and low paying jobs that often characterized a woman's position in India.

Source: Chen May Yee, "High-Tech Life for Indian's Women," *The Wall Street Journal*, November 1, 2001, p. B1.

....

derives from its large supply of well-trained, English-speaking workers, a powerful cost-quality combination. Second is its increasing ability to compete on speed of delivery. The "Made in India" brand is gaining equity as it offers services that stand for high quality and good value. Added to this is the return of Non-Resident Indians (NRI) to India, individuals drawn by entrepreneurial opportunities in India's IT sector. The brain drain, which has usually been Westward, is now showing some reversal to India's benefit. Many of the returning IT professionals have experience in the well-developed Western markets, and will able to bring back the fruits of their experience to India.

Challenges to Growth

Yet, in spite of the many successes in this area, India faces numerous obstacles to growth of the IT sector in the short to medium term. At the macro level, the government's plans for privatization and deregulation of key sectors, such as banking and telecommunications are slow and halting because the political process demands consensus on these issues from various groups at different levels. Many of the long-distance telecom providers are still under state-owned and -controlled international bandwidth, which is insufficient to meet the country's needs. In the domestic arena, lack of competition in telephone service translates to lack of phone lines and high rates for local access. In fact, *The Economist's The World in 2001* headlined its article on India "Impossible India's Improbable Chance." The author, David Gardner, wrote, "as even the most loyalist commentators could not fail to observe, it is hard to telephone around the corner." He suggests that much of the telecommunications potential has been overstated.

Clearly, expensive local phone rates could be a major deterrent to Internet use. The cost of Internet access is also relatively high since use is still metered. Lack of bandwidth for data also influences availability, cost, and speed of access. India's total international bandwidth is only 350MB, compared with China's 40GB and 200GB in the U.S.[9] Interruptions and fluctuation in the power supply further compound the problem creating another disincentive for growth of domestic Internet use and web-based retailing. A high quality, reliable, and uninterrupted supply of power is critical to the sector's growth. The domestic market for PCs is growing in India. However, critical factors for growth in business-to-consumer are a reliable delivery system, sufficient bandwidth for easy and fast access to data and graphics, and higher levels of credit card use to facilitate payment. In a report by the U.S. government to facilitate Internet development, five key principles were outlined in a document titled, "A Framework for Global Electronic Commerce." They included:

- Private sector leadership,
- Avoidance of undue restrictions,
- Establishment of a legal environment based on a contractual model of law,
- Recognition of the unique qualities of the Internet, and
- Facilitation of global e-commerce.[10]

The government of India, recognizing the urgency of the sector's growth to India's economic development, has stated its intention to follow many of the same principles set forth above in the U.S. government report.[11]

If information technology is to fuel India's economic growth into the ranks of the developed countries, there needs to be a confluence of policy changes. Ironically, the IT industry has thrived up to this point on government inattention. Now the visible hand of the government is directed at this fledgling industry with the seemingly benign intent of helping it grow. However, as the industry grows and matures, it faces bottlenecks in the form of inadequate power, weak telecommunications and transportation infrastructure, and perhaps an exhaustible supply of IT talent if educational institutions in India fail to rise to the challenge. In the critical area of power, for instance, leading Western firms entered India following liberalization. They were lured by the massive power shortages in the context of a growing economy. Now they are leaving India due to frustration with bureaucratic roadblocks, government pricing controls, which prevent them from earning fair market returns, and disillusionment with a difficult market.

A labor-skills shortage could short circuit the IT sector's growth, if the country does not take steps to deal with the issue on an urgent basis. As the global IT industry grows, there is a shortage of trained IT human resources internationally and developed countries increasingly turn to countries like India to recruit labor for their domestic markets. The workforce turnover in India is roughly 25 percent, compared with 18 percent in California. The shortage of trained and experienced IT human resources bids up the cost of labor, which could erase one of India's key advantages. India currently trains 68,000 software professionals a year and needs to have 2.2 million a year by 2008 to meet projected demand.

Conclusion

India's passage to the Internet economy could be blocked by "old economy" roadblocks. IT has no political, economic, or social boundaries and if India is to support development in this sector it has to create the right environment for growth. A slowdown in the Indian economy will further boost IT investment by old economy companies interested in increasing productivity. A slowdown in the U.S. economy could have a similar effect by opening new opportunities for Indian IT firms with their dual advantage of a proven track record and lower costs relative to the U.S.

McKinsey-NASSCOM Report on India's IT Sector[11]

The McKinsey-NASSCOM report published in 2000 makes the following recommendations for enabling the Indian IT industry's growth:

- Build a base of highly competitive "knowledge workers"
- Create a regulatory environment friendly to the IT sector
- Create India-based IT multinationals
- Build a world-class telecommunications infrastructure
- Build the "Made in India" brand for IT products
- Encourage entrepreneurship and new venture creation

According to the report, government should:

A labor-skills shortage could short circuit the IT sector's growth, if the country does not take steps to deal with the issue on an urgent basis.

- Improve infrastructure—education, telecommunications, transportation, and postal system
- Privatize and deregulate key sectors such as banking, telecommunications and power
- Allow foreign competition in areas formerly under State control.
- Cut bureaucracy and red tape to facilitate Foreign Direct Investment and entry of foreign firms
- Cut unproductive government subsidies for power and agriculture
- Increase government spending on infrastructure, primary education, and health
- Computerize governance mechanisms when possible
- Increase government accountability

NOTES

1. "Clinton's India visit to boost business," www.expressindia.com/ie/daily.

2. Gardner, David, "GE chief warns India," *Financial Times,* September 18, 2000, p. 3.

3. Taylor, Paul, "New Pioneers at the helm, Indian Information Technology, *Financial Times* Survey," July 4, 2000, p. III.

4. http://www.nasscom.org/template/itinindia.htm

5. Merchant, Khozem, "Defining the Indian software brand in a competitive world," *Financial Times-IT Review 14,* Indian IT and Communications, February 21, 2001, p. XIV.

6. http://www.ap-it.com/vision.html

7. Levander, Michelle, "By Its Bootstraps," *World Business, The Wall Street Journal,* September 25, 2000, p. R16.

8. "At India, H&Q tie up for VC fund" *The Economic Times,* November 21, 2000. http://www.economictimes.com

9. http://www.nua.ie/surveys

10. "The Emerging Digital Economy II," U.S. Department of Commerce, June 1999. (http://www.ecommerce.gov)

11. http://www.nasscom.org.

CHAPTER 15

Future Scenarios

FIRMS who seek to do business in the Indian market ultimately want to know what they can realistically expect in the future for this emerging market. In this section, we will describe some alternative scenarios for the Indian market, for both the short and long term.

On balance, our book paints a positive view of marketing opportunities in India. The more than 20 corporate executives we interviewed in depth as well as the firms surveyed while we were writing the book generally concurred. This should come as no surprise. If international trade is to continue to expand it must include the big emerging markets because the developed country markets with their flat or declining population bases cannot be the sole engines for expansion of the world economy.

That observation, however, has to be tempered by the fact that the world economy is slowing as this book goes to print. Clearly, September 11, 2001 is a factor but there is also the preoccupation with, among others, the Euro, Enron, the war on terrorism, and Japanese banking concerns, that are factors. Much also will depend on two key variables:

- First, the political stability and government policies that will be the determinants of how fast the Indian economy can grow. In a multiparty democracy with uneasy coalition politics, this is always a question.

- Second, Indian's relations with its neighbors in the region and the constant threat of military conflict and instability will have a bearing on the growth prospects for the market. In fact, India and Pakistan were on a military alert at the outset of 2002.

The following scenarios, therefore, represent a range of likely "outcomes" for the Indian economy from the "strongly favorable" to "strongly unfavorable." We have tried to formulate these scenarios from the viewpoint of a foreign firm seeking to enter or expand its operations in India.

Short Term

Optimistic: In the short term, the most favorable scenario is of a market that continues its economic liberalization policies, accelerates its market-opening measures, and simultaneously tackles the serious infrastructure problems in the areas of energy, transportation, and telecommunication. If this were to occur, in five to ten years the economy might have a realistic chance to grow at 7 to 8 percent a year. It is generally agreed that with that level of sustainable growth, India could start making the gains in per-capita income that can raise consumer consumption level while simultaneously reducing poverty levels. Unfortunately, the slowing of the world economy at the beginning of the millennium and the continuing lack of concerted action on the part of the government in New Delhi makes us believe this scenario is less likely.

Most Likely: A second short-term scenario, and one that we consider more likely, is that the economy will continue to make only modest gains with annual growth rates of 5 to 6 percent. While this could nevertheless present significant opportunities to foreign firms in many industries, it would mean India will still trail China in its ability to attract significant foreign investment and raise overall per-capita income. Based on our observations elsewhere in this book, this level of growth and the WTO-mandated changes in trade regimes will mean that several consumer products (e.g .packaged foods and household appliances) and services (e.g. financial and retail) will see significant opportunities.

Pessimistic: Our final and most pessimistic scenario is that the slowdown in the world economy and continued infrastructure problems, combined with the lack of political will to liberalize the economy would keep growth rates at 3 to 4 percent or less. This would certainly mean that the economy would lose ground in real terms and grow at or below the rate of inflation.

Barring any major shock to the world economy in the form of a long-lasting recession, we believe the Indian electorate expects better economic performance than this, based on the experience of the last decade and would find such performance unacceptable.

Of course, changes of government alone cannot ensure that any significant improvement in the economy will occur because in an increasingly integrated world economy, the fortunes of an individual country's economy are inevitably linked to those of all other economies. It does appear that the Asian economies have started to make a comeback and this bodes well for India.

Long Term

Constructing scenarios for the next 10 or 20 years and beyond is even harder, but we have constructed a range of possibilities that span an optimistic to a pessimistic continuum.

India is projected to be the most populated nation in the world by the year 2050. It needs to aim for growth rates that can make a significant dent in the overall level of poverty. Further, it has a simultaneous need to raise the average income of the overall population to a point at which the standard of living sustains consumption levels that present opportunities to foreign firms. The per capita income in India at the beginning of the new millennium is under US$400 in nominal terms and under US$1,200 in terms of purchasing power. Compare this with another large country in terms of population—Brazil. India's per-capita income is only about one-eighth that of Brazil's in nominal terms. In comparison with China, India's per-capita income is lower in terms of purchasing power parity. When you add to this the issue of uneven distribution of income, which also is an issue in Brazil, China, and other developed countries, you can see the extent of the challenge facing the Indian economy.

Optimistic: In our most optimistic scenario, we see the Indian economy sustaining growth rates of 7 or 8 percent annually over a period of several decades. However, remember that no economy has performed this well in recent times. China did manage double digit growth for an extended period during the 1980s and 1990s and the impressive growth of Chinese per-capita income is largely a consequence of this. The Chinese performance was based on a large manufacturing industry geared to low-end exports especially operating on an outsourced base for U.S. production and we have noted elsewhere that India is unlikely to follow that pattern.

The Indian plan calls for exports of software and software services to reach as much as US$50 billion by 2010. However, with the absence of a manufacturing base and the infrastructure that such manufacturing would demand, it is hard to see how any significant benefits of the software-export market would spill over to other sectors. Given the "messy" democratic processes of its government, the Indian economy is also unlikely to match the conviction of the Chinese regime as it went through its process of opening to the world economy. However, certain Indian states are likely to sustain a substantial growth ratio. In the end, therefore, we conclude that this optimistic scenario is unlikely. However, in our opinion, India's policy makers should aspire to this ideal.

Most Likely: The "middle" scenario would find the Indian economy growing at an average sustained rate of 5 percent. This would keep it on an upward trajectory, albeit one in which growth would be consumed by inflation and population growth. In this scenario too, we see a continued "divergence" between the rich and poor in both urban and rural areas. This scenario will provide attractive opportunities on a selective level to foreign firms which cater to the higher end of the market—a situation not unlike that seen more commonly in certain Latin American markets. The greater general difficulty of controlling population in a democratic regime will be the reason that India will likely overtake China in population with lower overall levels of literacy and opportunities for women, particularly in the lower income population.

Pessimistic: Our pessimistic long-term scenario sees the Indian market continuing the lackluster performance of the decades since independence with an average growth rate far short of the combined effects of inflation and population growth rate. The government will continue to "waffle" on major economic issues and not provide an adequate environment for development. In this scenario, the economy would struggle to attract foreign investment as it has over several decades. While this scenario is not entirely unlikely, we feel that it is less likely than the "middle" scenario above, and also that whatever its likelihood, it will not completely preclude attractive opportunities for foreign firms in the Indian market.

Summing Up

Foreign firms considering entering or expanding existing operations in the Indian market should not expect dramatic change to occur. At the same time, however, we expect the general opening of the Indian market to continue for the foreseeable future. This means there will be many opportunities on which firms can capitalize over the next decade or two.

Forecasts and scenarios for periods beyond the next 20 years are necessarily hard to make. However, barring major dislocations on a global or regional level, we think it is safe to assume that for the "unhurried" and patient investor or business firm, attractive opportunities should be available in the Indian market.

With its large English-speaking middle class, India also can act as a bellwether market to test for both products and employee talent which could then find application in other markets. As one of our executive interviewees told us, already foreign firms are developing new products and services customized for the Indian market with the eventual objective of expanding these to other foreign markets. They are also interested in moving executive personnel from India to other markets in both the developing and developed world.

India is a market that bears watching. For the firm looking at the long-term, this is a good time to establish a toehold in a largely untapped giant market.

Updating Our Scenarios

As we move further into the 21st century, it will be in the reader's best interest to continually evaluate which of the above future scenarios seem to be the most appropriate. We offer here an India Analysis Chart which may assist readers in determining the direction the country is taking today.

India Analysis Chart

Positives	Large middle class, English spoken, space capability, privatization starting, WTO commitment, new Foreign Direct Investment rules, software sector, strong higher education and research abilities, satellite and cable TV systems, state government powers.
Negatives	Remaining trade barriers, relations with Pakistan, nuclear military threat, political risk rating, religious divisions, classic bureaucracy, corruption (all levels), weak infrastructure (power, roads, air), poor intellectual property protection, weak bankruptcy laws, inefficient tax structure, size of public sector, weak central government, poverty.
Watching	Kashmir (Pakistan border conflict), China and Sri Lanka relations, distribution channel development (rural areas), commitment to economic development, effectiveness of coalition government, success of current multinational corporations, attempts to solve energy issues.

Changes in any of the categories can be important indicators of the future potential of this major market. Naturally, if some of the Negatives become Positives, such as a reduction in public sector employment or the creation of better intellectual property protection, we would assess things differently. However, we suggest that the reader look especially at the "Watching" section to see if any of these critical considerations move toward either the Positives or the Negatives. For example, a stronger commitment by the Indian government to economic development or an end to the conflict in Kashmir could dramatically improve the country's potential and its attractiveness to foreign investors.

Ten Questions

Here are a few questions we suggest executives ask as they evaluate the Indian market:

- Has India (or its individual states) taken real steps to solve its infrastructure problems in general and its power and road problems in particular?

- Have India and Pakistan forged an agreement to end the conflict in Kashmir? This is important in reducing the arms race and reducing military costs for India and Pakistan.

- Has India moved forward on privatization? You will know the answer if it has furthered privitization of such critical sectors as airlines and banking, thereby signaling that it is serious about reducing the bloated public sector.

- Has India moved directly to eliminate all remaining trade barriers, including quotas, and to fully accept the WTO's trade intent?

- Has India developed strong intellectual property protection and is it being enforced?

- Have the major global retailing giants, including ones such as Wal-Mart and Carrefour, begun to operate in India? This is an important signal in the development of distribution channels.

- Has India's central government moved to end corruption, strengthen its bankruptcy laws, make needed corrections in its stock markets, and improve the tax structure? Any one or all of these would indicate a strengthening of the government's will to make needed changes.

- Has India's political risk rating improved enough to place it in line with developed economies?

- Are U.S., Canadian and European multinational corporations beginning to report a series of "successes" in India? This often is best measured by whether they expand in a country and whether they increase their level of ownership.

- Has the software sector continued to expand and are more and more bright young Indian professionals staying at home instead of looking for better opportunities in Europe, the U.S., Brazil, and elsewhere?

A positive answer to three to five of these ten questions would dramatically improve India's attraction for foreign investors.

India's Retailing Comes of Age

The McKinsey Quarterly, 2000 Number 4 Asia

Reprinted with permission

Michael Fernandes, Chandrika Gadi, Amit Khanna, Palash Mitra, and Subbu Narayanswamy

The "licensing raj" has long kept the doors of India's retail market closed to large domestic operators and to outsiders. But the doors are now opening.

As citizens of the world's largest democracy, Indians are trusted to choose their own government. But, until recently, they were not free to choose what they wanted to buy. A paternalistic regime of control manifested itself in licensing laws that restricted the production of consumer goods and in regulations that limited the size of manufacturing plants. A lack of incentives held back investments to develop new products. Multinational companies were kept out, and imports were throttled by tariffs often exceeding 200 percent. The result was that Indians could buy any car as long as it was a Morris Oxford or a Fiat, any toothpaste as long as it was Colgate, any watch as long as it came from HMT, and any radio as long as it was produced by Philips.

Now, however, market liberalization and increasingly assertive consumers are sowing the seeds of a retail transformation that will bring

The authors wish to acknowledge the contributions of Arati Sood and Amnit Dhillon.
Michael Fernandes, Palash Mitra, and Subbu Narayanswamy *are consultants in McKinsey's Mumbai office;* Chandrika Gadi and Amit Khanna *are consultants in the Delhi office.*

bigger Indian and multinational operators on to the scene. Although the rewards might not be instant, there are tremendous opportunities in such a huge market, worth a total of $20 billion a year in India's four largest cities—Mumbai, Delhi, Calcutta, and Chennai (in descending order of size)—and $180 billion overall.[1] A number of Indian and international retailers are entering this nascent market. To do so, they are being forced to build their supply chains from scratch and to spur consumer interest in products that aren't familiar to many Indian shoppers. For example, McDonald's, which has spent more than five years developing a supply chain and devising a nonbeef menu, is now emerging as a force in the fast-food market.

The impact of liberalization

India is the last large Asian economy to liberalize its retail sector. In Thailand, more than 40 percent of all consumer goods are sold through supermarkets, convenience stores, and department stores. A similar phenomenon has swept through Malaysia, Taiwan, Thailand, and Indonesia. Even in China, more than a tenth of all consumer goods are sold through modern retail formats—a proportion that is growing rapidly (Exhibit 1).

1. Operations Research Group (ORG), an Indian research organization.

EXHIBIT 1 Out with the old, in with the new
Percent of retail sales, by format, 1997

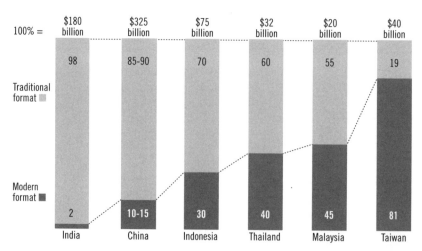

Source: Euromonitor International.

But in India, the development of an organized retail industry was stymied by the "licensing raj." The grocery business, for instance, has been dominated by small father-and-son stores with fixed prices set by manufacturers under government direction. In no category was there scope for an organized chain to develop any advantage—whether of price, range, or service—over the unorganized competitors that typically operated with family labor on their own property. The impact of regulation on choice and quality was evident in the encyclopedic shopping lists that family and friends presented to Indians going abroad. The lengthy requests meant that they traveled light going out but exceedingly heavy coming back, weighed down by toiletries, medicines, perfumes, underwear, chocolates, and Scotch whisky.

It may soon be possible for Indian vacationers to travel light in both directions. The government is cutting back on licensing and permitting the construction of bigger factories. The quality of local goods is improving as Indian manufacturers upgrade their production for export markets. Customs duties are dropping, and there is a shift from quota-based to tariff-based systems. Import restrictions aimed at multinationals have been removed in nearly all sectors, letting in Sony and Samsung in durable goods and Kellogg in consumer goods, to mention only a few of the contenders. Categories such as biscuits, dairy products, juices, and personal-care products are following suit. A survey by the Operations Research Group, an Indian research organization, found that 19 consumer goods categories, with 1,378 brands and 2,579 individual products, entered the Indian retail market from 1990 to 1996.

At least one fly remains in the ointment, however. In contrast to the rest of Asia, where international retailers are welcomed, India hasn't made the development of its retail sector a priority. Foreign investment doesn't receive automatic approval, and retailers must show that they are adding value—by, say, making some products in India rather than just buying and selling goods there. Lobbying by small retailers has perpetuated this barrier. In addition, regulations restricting real-estate purchases remain, along with a tax regime that favors smaller retail businesses.

Dealing with the strategic issues

In approaching the Indian market, retailers must come to grips with four factors: the characteristics of particular sectors, local talent, geographical reach, and integration of on-line and physical offerings.

1. Look for an attractive sector

EXHIBIT 2   India's retail sectors fall into 3 categories

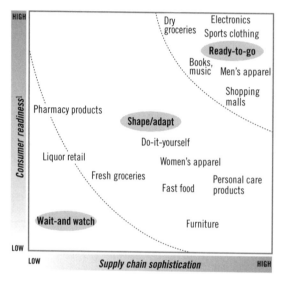

1 Degree to which consumer is comfortable with modern formats, willing to buy packed, chilled, prepared, or ready-made foods, and willing to pay for added value.

Retail sectors in India fall into three categories (Exhibit 2). The first, "ready-to-go," comprises several subcategories in which determined retailers can build positions immediately because ease of sourcing, the proliferation of products, and consumer acceptance have reached a level that permits the exploitation of advantages of scale and range. These ready-to-go sectors include dry groceries (grains and cereals, packaged foods, toiletries, and household items), electronics (see sidebar "Electronics"),

---

Electronics

One "ready-to-go" sector is electronics. Its growth has been enhanced by reductions in import duties and a move away from quota-based imports, and margins have increased as competition for shelf space intensifies—though margins are even narrower on regular brands (8 to 10 percent) than they are in developed markets (15 percent). A few retailers have already begun to capture the opportunity. The Indian company Viveks, for example, has 26 stores in southern India, annual sales of $40 million, and big expansion plans.

As in developed markets, chain retailers must contrive to boost their margins on new and irregular products and to keep overheads low. The ability to manage secondhand sales in second-tier towns and rural markets would also be an advantage, since many products are sold on an exchange basis (that is, old for new, with a rebate). Eventually, retailers should aim to move up the value chain and build margins through innovative sourcing (for example, tapping global supplies at a discount), the sale of accessories, and the provision of services.

certain kinds of men's clothing (see sidebar "Clothing"), books and music, and shopping malls.

Clothing

India's $3.5 billion urban clothing market is the country's second-largest opportunity for organized retailers. But the low penetration of brands (20 percent of the market) and the popularity of traditional clothing (30 percent) conspire to make this a difficult market to enter. Despite these problems, certain market slivers are both potentially profitable and amenable to change.

Of the various subcategories within clothing, men's ready-to-wear and sports clothing are "ready to go." The market for men's clothing is estimated to be worth $2 billion a year. Branded ready-to-wear garments already account for 40 percent of these purchases—double the share of branded items in the overall clothing market. This market segment is growing by more than 30 percent a year.

The proliferation of brands creates an opportunity for multibrand outlets to capture a larger slice of business. Men's clothing is therefore one of the strongest categories in most department stores. The arrival of Adidas, Nike, and Reebok five years ago was marked by the opening throughout India of showrooms intended to create an awareness of the products and to show people how to use them. The time is ripe for these brands, along with Indian "wannabes" such as Liberty, to develop multibrand sports clothing and footwear stores that meet the needs of serious sportsmen and fashion-conscious people alike.

If anything could unravel a clothes retailer's plans, it is women's clothing. First, women's wear in India consists of two distinct outfits, the sari and the salwar kameez; Western clothing is likely to remain a niche market for college students in urban markets and a relatively small number of women executives. Second, standardized clothing is anathema to the Indian woman; she wants the cloth, cut, and finish to be unique. For these reasons, manufacturing continues to be dominated by small-scale outfits that offer a bewildering array of fabric designs and patterns as well as an army of tailors who cater to individual tastes.

The difficulty of building a strong retail business in women's clothing is the single most irksome bottleneck in the development of clothing superstores and department stores because women are the main buyers, even of men's clothes. Matters are made worse for retailers by the low use of cosmetics and toiletries. Per capita consumption of cosmetics in India is a paltry 10 cents a year, compared with $2 in Thailand and $3.10 in Mexico. Lipstick and facial makeup are used in only 15 and 1.5 percent of Indian households, respectively.

But as the proportion of working women in India rises—and, with it, incomes—it will become possible for chains to serve the needs of these women profitably, a trend that has now begun to be observed in Mumbai, India's most cosmopolitan city. Such chains will have a high dependence on men's clothing and casual and sports wear, and they will be concentrated in upmarket urban centers.

Dry groceries are particularly attractive because the proliferation of brands and products has helped improve retail margins on two levels: packaged-goods companies must offer retailers better terms to obtain shelf space, and retailers can trade consumers up to goods of higher value. Upmarket supermarkets such as FoodWorld are seducing customers with frozen foods and a superior range of goods; discount grocers such as Subhiksha attract customers on the strength of the generous discounts they can offer because of their increased margin spread. Collectively, these kinds of stores have captured nearly 20 percent of the dry-grocery retail market in the southern city of Chennai since 1997.

The second category of retailing, "shape/adapt," includes fresh groceries (see sidebar "Fresh groceries"), women's clothing, do-it-yourself

---

Fresh Groceries

The supply chain for fresh foods in India is currently quite rudimentary; investment in refrigeration has been limited, and there are few large-scale food processors. As yet, there is no way to offer customers standardized produce throughout a retail chain, and wastage of up to 30 percent across a chain is common. Even so, a retailer willing to invest could build a highly profitable business, although it would have to be built from scratch.

In addition to the difficulties of sourcing, there is the fact that Indians are still not ready to get fresh fruit and vegetables from a supermarket. Most prefer to buy fresh produce every day precisely because it is fresh and because they are short of refrigerator space. Moreover, mobile street vendors, who bring fresh produce to the doorstep, offer a convenient way to purchase these items. Town and city dwellers are beginning to show a willingness to buy from stores that are cleaner and better stocked and that provide nonseasonal produce, but their prices must be competitive.

Where meat is concerned, Indians have an additional reason for their reluctance to buy from a supermarket. Contrary to popular perception, more than 70 percent of them eat meat. Customers choose their chicken and fish live, and mutton is slaughtered at the shop. Meat markets are usually separate from produce and grocery markets, since vegetarians may be unwilling to shop for their food in places that sell meat.

Given the special characteristics of dry and fresh groceries, supermarkets emphasizing popular dry goods and some fresh foods will probably be the dominant retail format, at least initially. Except in a few big cities, hypermarkets would be feasible only as part of the second wave of retail evolution. Warehouse clubs could emerge to serve the multitude of small traders and restaurants as well as strong community groups and societies.

products, fast food, and furniture. Retailers in these sectors must invest substantially to shape the supply chain and persuade consumers to change their buying behavior.

The third category of retail segments, "wait and watch," comprises undeveloped sectors that provide no immediate opportunity for retailers. Pharmacy products and retail liquor products are two examples of such sectors. Low levels of over-the-counter drug purchases and complicated regulations make pharmacy chains unattractive. Liquor retailing will not take off, because of the stringent and varying regulation of alcohol in each Indian state.

2. Seek local talent

Building contacts is crucial to the success of any retail endeavor. A do-it-yourself business, for example, would have to create a sourcing chain by developing many small-scale local manufacturers and a network of contractors. Consumer goods companies—Indian or multinational—would be the best recruiting ground for managers ready to undertake this work. Such firms, traditionally the employer of choice for Indian business graduates, have the greatest experience in logistics management and in marketing to the Indian consumer.

3. Consider how far to reach

About 40 percent of India's high-income urban population lives in Mumbai, Delhi, Calcutta, Chennai, and Bangalore (Exhibit 3). This fact raises the question of whether it is necessary to go beyond these cities to capture the value of the Indian market.

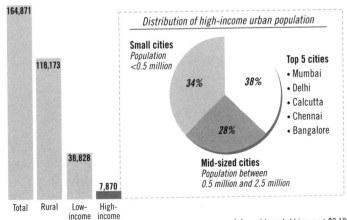

EXHIBIT 3 Urban markets are attractive
Thousands of households, 1996

Distribution of high-income urban population

164,871
118,173
38,828
7,870

Total | Rural | Low-income urban | High-income urban[1]

Small cities
Population <0.5 million

34%   38%

28%

Mid-sized cities
Population between 0.5 million and 2.5 million

Top 5 cities
• Mumbai
• Delhi
• Calcutta
• Chennai
• Bangalore

1 Annual household income ≥$2,100.
Source: National Council of Applied Economic Research (NCAER).

The answer is that for most retail formats, penetrating this handful of markets would be challenge enough during the first five years of operation. Clothing stores, convenience stores, and financial-services retailers—formats aimed at high-income groups—would have no need to reach beyond the 20 or 25 largest cities (those with populations greater than a million). More basic categories such as groceries and gasoline, though, might find value in entering second-tier cities, where there is little competition.

4. Integrate on-line and physical offerings

A savvy retailer breaking into India will build e-commerce into its business plan. True, personal computers will remain scarce. But ongoing investment in bandwidth, the development of shared Internet facilities, and the explosion in dot-com start-ups are expected to create a large base of users and shoppers (Exhibit 4).

Retailers entering the market need to take note of this force and determine how best to integrate an on-line offering with a bricks-and-mortar presence. At the outset, this is likely to be an issue mainly for booksellers and travel agencies—areas in which home delivery is important. But almost all types of retailers can proceed with their e-tailing plans without fear of cannibalization, the restructuring of the logistics network, or an attacker. In India, they are the attackers.

India remains one of the last frontiers of modern retailing. Conquering the country will always be a challenge, given the problems of the supply chain and consumer readiness as well as the prodigious complexities of so vast a market. But a retailer capable of simultaneously shap-

EXHIBIT 4 Internet use is on the rise
Thousands of internet users

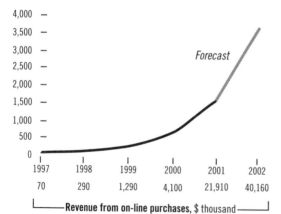

	1997	1998	1999	2000	2001	2002
	70	290	1,290	4,100	21,910	40,160

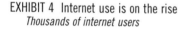

Revenue from on-line purchases, $ thousand

Source: International Data Corporation.

ing the market and adapting to its unique characteristics is likely to reap rewards that normally accrue only to those taking the first plunge into unknown territory. When Indians go shopping in the future, they will have almost as many choices as they do when they walk into a polling booth.

Resources

In the United States:

U.S. India Business Council
1615 H Street, NW
Washington, DC 20062-2000
Tel: (202) 463-5492
e-mail: usibc@uschamber.com

U.S. Department of Commerce
International Trade Administration
India Desk
Room 2308
14th & Constitution Avenues, NW
Washington, DC 20230
Tel: (202) 482-2954

The U.S. Commercial Service, an export service of the U.S. Department of Commerce, provides several different kinds of services to U.S. companies that wish to export to India. Market entry services include Gold Key, to schedule appointments with potential partners, licensees, distributors, and government contracts. Platinum Key is designed for companies that require long-term, sustained customized assistance with issues ranging from identifying markets and launching products to assistance on regulatory or technical matters. Video Gold Key Service allows

U.S. exporters to meet "virtually" face-to-face with customers and trade experts around the world. For a more detailed description of services, got to www.usatrade.gov or call 1-800-USA TRAD (872-8723) to obtain the name of the office nearest you. Also, see below for contact information in India.

In India

India is 10.5 hours ahead of eastern standard time in the United States.

The country code is 91
Codes for largest cities
Banglaore 80
Mumbai 22
Kolkata 33
Hyderabad 40
New Delhi 11

U.S. & Foreign Commercial Service
Telephone+ 91 (11) 331-6841 to 6849
e-mail: New. Delhi.Office.Box@mail.doc.gov

This U.S. government office in New Delhi is a good place to begin in India to be introduced to potential business partners, promote your products and services, and, and help you find the services you need.

Associated Chambers of Commerce
Allahabad Bank Building
17 Parliament Street
New Delhi 110 001
Tel: + 91 (11) 310-749

Chief Controller of Imports and Exports
Ministry of Commerce
Udyog Bhawan
Maulana Azad Road
New Delhi 110 001
Tel: + 91 (11) 301 1938

Confederation of Indian Industries
23-26 Institutional Area
Lodhi Road
New Delhi 110 003
Tel: + 91 (11) 462-9994

Export Import Bank of India
Centre One, Floor 21
World Trade Centre
Cuffe Parade
Mumbai 400 005
Tel: + 91 (22) 218-5277

Foreign Investment Promotion Board
Prime Minister's Secretariat
South Block
New Delhi 110 011
Tel: + 91 (11) 301-7839

India Investment Centre
Jeevan Vihar Building
Sansad Marg
New Delhi 110 001
Tel: + 91 (11) 312-622

Directorate-General of Commercial Intelligence and Statistics
1 Council House Street
Calcutta 800 001
Tel: + 91 (33) 283-111

Selected On-line Resources

All sites were checked and working as this book went to press.

India-Web: Business
Contains information on currency rates, banks, investment resources, business news, and links to other business resources
www.india-web.com/businessf.htm

U.S.–India Business Council
www.usibc.com

Trade India
Extensive business contacts in all types of categories as well as links to publications that are helpful in learning about Indian business requirements
www.TRADE-INDIA.com

National Informatics Center
www.nic.in

Government of India: Directory of Official Web Sites
http://goidirectory.nic.in

The Hindu
Online edition of India's national newspaper
www.hinduonline.com

India-Business Customs, Protocol, and Etiquette
A series of reports on business customs, protocol, negotiating, social customs, social etiquette, gift-giving, business entertainment, business travel. Downloadable at reasonable prices.
www.worldbiz.com/india.html

Hindustan Times
www.hindustantimes.com

Indiaworld
www.indiaworld.co.in

Times of India

On line edition of an English language newspaper published in New Delhi

www.timesofindia.com

Selected Market Research Firms in India

ACNielsen International Research
Citi Tower, 2nd Floor
61 Dr. S.S. Rao Road
Parel Mumbai 400 012
Tel: + 91 (22) 415-8029
e-mail: acnindia@giasbm01.vsnl.net.in

The Blackstone Group
Hotel Avion, Opp. Santacruz Airport
Nehru Road, Vile Parle (E)
Mumbai 400 057
Tel: + 91 (22) 618-2468
e-mail: bstoneb@bom3.vsnl.com

Indian Market Research Bureau
"A" Wing, Mhatre Pen Building
Senapati Bapat Road, Dadar
Mumbai 400 028
Tel: + 91 (22) 342-3500
e-mail: thomas.puliyel@imrbint.com

NFO MBL India Private Ltd.
Plot No. 17, Road No. 3
Banjara Hills
Hyderabad (A.P.) 500 034
Tel: + 91 (40) 335-5433
e-mail:mblindia@hd2.dot.net.in

Org-Marg Research, Inc.
30th floor, Centre One
World Trade centre Complex
Cuffe Parade
Mumbai 400 005
Tel: + 91 (22) 218-6922
e-mail:omrhq@vsnl.com

Quantum Market Research Pvt. Lt.
3096, HAL II Stage
Bangalore 560 038
Tel: +91 (80) 529-7548
e-mail: qmrl@giasbg01.vsnl.net.in

Taylor Sofres Mode (Mode Research Pvt., Ltd.)
15 Mayfair Road
Kolkata 700 019
Tel: + 91 (33) 247-2869
e-mail: modecal@cal.vsnl.net.in

Market-related Associations

Association of Advertising Agencies of India
Kevin Marshall, Executive Secretary
35, Maker Tower "F"
Cuffe Parade
Mumbai 400-005
Tel: 91 22 218 2164

Direct Marketing Association India
Bedeshwar
Gujarat 361 002
Tel: +91 (288) 559 135
e-mail:dmai@bigfoot.com

Franchising Association of India (FAI)
Mr. C. Yoginder Pal
1-C, Vulcan Insurance Bldg.
Churchgate, Mumbai 400-020
Tel: 91 22 282 1413

India Direct Selling Association (ISDA)
ISDA Secretariat
A-12 (Opp. A1116) Vasant Vihar
New Delhi
Tel: 91 11 615 2045

NASSCOM
International Youth Centre
Teen Murti Marg
Chanakyapuri
New Delhi 110-021
Tel: 91 11 301 0199

Index

About the Authors

ARUNA CHANDRA is an assistant professor of management at Indiana State University. Educated in India and the United States, she earned a B.A. in English from Women's Christian College in Madras, an M.A. in English and Linguistics from Bangalore University, and an MBA in Strategy and International Business at Kent State University. She holds two doctoral degrees in Strategy/International Business and English from Kent State University. Her teaching and research interests are in the areas of international management, entrepreneurship, and business strategy in emerging markets. She has assisted several small-to mid-sized firms in their export market development efforts to big emerging markets such as India. Dr. Chandra is a member of the Academy of International Business and the Academy of Management. She has published in several journals, including *The International Executive, Foreign Trade Review, Marketing Management,* and *The International Journal of Advertising.* E-mail: bssaruna@befac.indstate.edu.

PRADEEP RAU is a Professor of Marketing at The George Washington University, where he was chairman of the Department of Marketing from 1995 to 2000. His teaching and research interests are in international marketing, marketing research, and marketing strategy. He has numerous publications in professional business and academic journals and one book, *Marketing Strategies for the New Europe.*

Dr. Rau's international teaching experiences include the University of Aarhus in Denmark, Institute Tadbiran Awam Negara in Malaysia, University of International Business and Economics in Beijing, China, and several institutions in India including the Indian Institute of Technology, Delhi and the Indian Institutes of Management in Ahmedabad and Bangalore. He earned his Bachelor's of Technology at the Indian Institute of Technology in Kanpur, his MBA at the Indian Institute of Management at Calcutta, and his DBA at Kent State University.

JOHN K. RYANS, JR. is the Bridgestone Professor of International Business and Marketing at Kent State University. He has served as visiting professor at Columbia University and the University of Houston. He received his doctorate from Indiana University. He is a fellow of the Academy of International Business, and on the Executive Committee of the U.S. Department of Commerce's Northern Ohio District Export Council.

Dr. Ryans has written extensively in the fields of international business, marketing, and strategy, including more than 20 books and 200 articles in business journals, including the *Harvard Business Review*. He is the co-author with Dr. Rau, *Marketing Strategies for the New Europe*, published in 1990. He has served as a consultant to many U.S. and foreign manufacturing firms and advertising agencies, including Goodyear International, Xerox, The Interpublic Group, Novo Industries (Denmark), Master Builders, DEC, McCann-Erickson and the Bates Group.